Rimini (Italy) Travel Guide

A Complete Guide on When to Go, Where to Go and What to Do in The City Of Rimini, Italy

By

Lucas E. Glasse

Copyright

No part of this publication may be reproduced, distributed or transmitted in any way, including by photocopying, recording, or using an information storage and retrieval system, or by email, without permission from the publisher.

Copyright © 2023 Lucas E. Glasse
All rights reserved.

Disclaimer

The author and publisher have made every effort to ensure the accuracy of the information in this publication, but they are not responsible for any errors, omissions, or different interpretations of the material.

The following travel guide is intended to provide general information and recommendations for your convenience. However, it is important to note that travel experiences can vary, and circumstances may change beyond our control. We strive to provide accurate and up-to-date information, but we cannot guarantee the completeness, accuracy, or reliability of the content.

Please be aware that travel involves certain inherent risks, and it is your responsibility to exercise caution, conduct your own research, and make informed decisions regarding your travel plans. We strongly advise you to consult with relevant authorities, such as travel agencies, government advisories, and local authorities, to obtain the most current and accurate information regarding travel destinations, safety precautions, visa requirements, health risks, and any other factors that may impact your travel experience.

We disclaim any liability for any loss, injury, inconvenience, or damage arising from your reliance on the information provided in this travel guide. You undertake any travel activities at your own risk and assume full responsibility for your actions and decisions.

Please note that the recommendations, suggestions, and opinions expressed in this guide are based on our own experiences and subjective perspectives. Your preferences, individual circumstances, and personal judgment may differ, so we encourage you to use this guide as a starting point and tailor your travel plans accordingly.

Remember to secure appropriate travel insurance, follow local laws and regulations, respect local customs and cultures, and exercise personal judgment in all situations. Stay informed, stay safe, and enjoy your travel adventures responsibly.

Table of Contents

CHAPTER 1
INTRODUCTION/OVERVIEW
- About Rimini
  - Geography
    - Physical Features:
    - The Coastline and Beaches:
    - Historical Landmarks:
  - Climate
    - Weather Patterns:
    - Seasons
      - Spring (March to May)
      - Summer (June to August)
      - Autumn (September to November)
      - Winter (December to February)
    - Climate Change
      - Temperature Increase
      - Precipitation Patterns
      - Sea-Level Rise
  - Official Language Of Rimini/Other Languages
  - Rimini's Official Currency
  - System Of Government
  - Brief History Of Rimini
    - Ancient Times
    - Middle Ages:
    - Renaissance and Modern Era
    - World War II and Modern Developments
    - Tourism

- Why Visit Rimini

CHAPTER 2

ESSENTIALS FOR YOUR TRIP TO RIMINI
- Ideal Time To Visit Rimini
  - Summer (June to August)
  - Spring (March to May)
  - Autumn (September to November)
  - Winter (December to February)
  - For Budget-conscious Visitors
    - Spring (March to May)
    - Autumn (September to November)
- Visas And Documents Requirements (If Visiting From Outside Italy)
  - Visa Requirements
    - Tourist Visa (Schengen Visa)
    - Other Visa Types
      - Work Visa
      - Student Visa
      - Business Visa
      - Family Reunification Visa
      - Study Abroad or Exchange Program Visa
      - Long-Term Visa or Residence Permit
  - Valid Passport
  - Travel Insurance
  - Proof of Accommodation
  - Proof of Sufficient Funds
  - Return Ticket
  - Additional Documents
- What To Pack For Your Trip To Rimini

- Clothing
- Footwear
- Accessories
- Toiletries
- Electronics
- Miscellaneous Items

Getting To Rimini
- By Plane
- By Train
  - Train From Outside Italy
- By Bus
  - Bus From Outside Italy
- By Car
- By Boat
  - Ferries to nearby ports
  - Cruises

Getting Around Rimini
- Bus
- Train
- Bicycle
- Walking
- Taxi
- What About Ride Sharing Services?

Accommodations In Rimini (Where To Stay In Rimini)
- Hotels And Resorts
- Bed And Breakfasts
- Vacation Rentals And Apartments
- Budget And Hostel Options

　　　　Unique Stays And Luxury Retreats
CHAPTER 3
WHAT TO DO IN RIMINI
　　Must See Landmarks
　　Iconic Museums And Galleries (In And Near Rimini)
　　Natural Wonders And Parks
　　Historic Sites And Architecture
　　Hidden Gems And Local Favorites
　　Family Friendly Activities In Rimini
　　Day Trips And Excursions From Rimini
　　Rimini's Festivals And Carnivals
　　Nightlife In Rimini
CHAPTER 4
DINING IN RIMINI
　　Dining Options
　　　　Restaurants
　　　　Trattorias
　　　　Pizzerias
　　　　Seafood Restaurants
　　Rimini's Cuisines
　　Best Bars In Rimini
CHAPTER 5
SHOPPING IN RIMINI
　　Popular Shopping Areas
　　Souvenirs and Local Crafts
　　Fashion and Design
　　Markets and Flea Markets
　　Specialty Stores and Boutiques

CHAPTER 6
OTHER PRACTICAL INFORMATION
Money Matters
Currency
Money Exchange
ATMs
Credit Cards
Language and Communication
Language
Useful Phrases
Travel Insurance and Health Concerns
Travel Insurance
Health Concerns
Safety and Security
Travel Warnings
Emergency Contacts
CHAPTER 7
CONCLUSION
Additional Resources

CHAPTER 1

INTRODUCTION/OVERVIEW

Welcome to the "Rimini Travel Guide 2023"! Whether you're a beach lover, a history enthusiast, or a foodie looking for a new culinary adventure, Rimini has something for everyone. Situated on the stunning Adriatic coast of Italy, this vibrant city is known for its beautiful beaches, ancient ruins, lively nightlife, and delicious cuisine.

In this travel guide, we'll provide you with all the essential information you need to plan an unforgettable trip to Rimini in 2023. From the must-visit attractions to hidden gems, from the best time to visit to local customs and traditions, we've got you covered. Let's dive into the rich history, cultural experiences, and natural beauty that Rimini has to offer.

About Rimini

In this section about Rimini, we will delve into revealing facts and important things to know about the place. Let's explore some interesting details:

Geography

Located on the eastern coast of Italy, Rimini is a beautiful city that captivates visitors with its stunning beaches, historical treasures, and vibrant atmosphere. With a strategic location along the Adriatic Sea, Rimini has been an important maritime hub since ancient times.

Physical Features:

Rimini is situated in the Emilia-Romagna region, in the province of Rimini, and is part of the Riviera Romagnola. It lies on a flat coastal plain, surrounded by rolling hills and the Apennine Mountains in the distance. The city is bordered by the Marecchia River to the north and the Ausa River to the south, providing a natural boundary and adding to the scenic charm of the area.

The Coastline and Beaches:

Rimini boasts a breathtaking coastline that stretches for approximately 15 kilometers along the Adriatic Sea. The sandy beaches of Rimini are renowned for their pristine beauty and offer a variety of amenities and services for beachgoers. The beaches are divided into numerous bathing establishments, known as "bagni," which provide sunbeds, umbrellas, restaurants, and recreational activities. Visitors can enjoy sunbathing, swimming in the azure waters, or engaging in water sports such as sailing, windsurfing, and jet skiing.

Historical Landmarks:

Beyond its stunning coastline, Rimini is steeped in history and boasts a wealth of historical landmarks. The city was founded by the Romans in 268 BCE and was a crucial center along the ancient Roman road Via Flaminia, connecting Rome to the northern regions of Italy. Rimini's most iconic landmark is the Arch of Augustus, a triumphal arch dating back to 27 BCE, which stands as a testament to the city's Roman past. Other notable landmarks include the Tiberius Bridge, a remarkable Roman bridge over the Marecchia River, and the Malatesta Temple, an exquisite Renaissance church.

Rimini's geography encompasses a stunning coastline, picturesque countryside, and a rich historical heritage. The combination of beautiful beaches, historical landmarks, and a favorable climate make Rimini a year-round destination for travelers seeking both relaxation and cultural exploration. Whether you're strolling along the sandy shores, admiring ancient Roman architecture, or exploring the charming countryside, Rimini offers a diverse and enchanting experience that leaves visitors with lasting memories of this coastal gem in Italy.

Climate

Climate of Rimini: A Detailed Overview of Weather Patterns, Seasons, and Climate Change

Rimini, a beautiful coastal city located in the Emilia-Romagna region of Italy, is known for its stunning beaches, vibrant nightlife, and historical landmarks. The city experiences a Mediterranean climate, characterized by mild winters and hot, dry summers. In this article, we will delve into the detailed climatic conditions of Rimini, exploring its weather patterns, seasons, and the potential impacts of climate change on the region.

Weather Patterns:

Rimini's climate is heavily influenced by its coastal location along the Adriatic Sea. The sea acts as a moderating factor, helping to keep temperatures relatively mild throughout the year. The city experiences a Mediterranean microclimate, with distinct seasonal variations.

Seasons

Spring (March to May)

Spring in Rimini is characterized by mild temperatures, with average highs ranging from 14°C (57°F) in March to 21°C (70°F) in May. The region experiences moderate rainfall during this season, with occasional showers and blossoming flora.

Summer (June to August)

Summers in Rimini are hot and dry, with average temperatures ranging from 24°C (75°F) in June to 29°C (84°F) in August. July and August are the hottest months, with temperatures occasionally reaching above 30°C (86°F). The sea breeze provides some relief from the heat, making the beaches popular destinations during this time.

Autumn (September to November)

Autumn in Rimini brings milder temperatures, with average highs ranging from 23°C (73°F) in September to 16°C (61°F) in November. The region experiences sporadic rainfall, and the surrounding hillsides showcase beautiful fall foliage.

Winter (December to February)

Winters in Rimini are relatively mild compared to other parts of Italy. Average temperatures range from 9°C (48°F) in December to 11°C (52°F) in February. While snowfall is rare, occasional cold spells can bring temperatures close to freezing.

Climate Change

Like many other regions globally, Rimini is also experiencing the impacts of climate change. Rising temperatures, changing precipitation patterns, and sea-level rise are some of the key concerns for the city's climate future.

Temperature Increase

Over the past few decades, Rimini has witnessed a gradual increase in average temperatures. Heatwaves during the summer months have become more frequent and intense, affecting tourism, agriculture, and overall comfort levels for residents and visitors.

Precipitation Patterns

Climate change has influenced precipitation patterns in Rimini. While the overall annual rainfall may not have changed significantly, the distribution and intensity of rainfall events have become more erratic. This can lead to increased risks of flooding in some areas and drought in others.

Sea-Level Rise

Rimini's coastal location makes it susceptible to the consequences of rising sea levels. Increased erosion, storm surges, and saltwater intrusion into freshwater sources are potential challenges the city may face in the future.

Rimini's climate offers a pleasant Mediterranean experience, with warm summers, mild winters, and distinct seasons. However, the region is not immune to the impacts of climate change. Understanding the changing weather patterns and potential risks is crucial for policymakers, residents, and visitors to adapt and mitigate the effects of climate change in Rimini. Through sustainable practices and proactive measures, Rimini can continue to thrive while preserving its natural beauty and resilience in the face of a changing climate.

Official Language Of Rimini/Other Languages

The official language of Rimini is Italian. Italian is the national language of Italy and is spoken by the majority of the population. It is the language used in government, education, media, and daily life.

In addition to Italian, there may be other languages spoken in Rimini due to the city's diverse population and tourism industry. English is often spoken and understood in tourist areas and by those working in the hospitality industry. Additionally, there may be residents or visitors who speak other languages such as German, French, Spanish, or Russian.

However, it's important to note that Italian remains the primary language used in official capacities in Rimini and throughout Italy.

Rimini's Official Currency

Italy's official currency is the Euro (€). The Euro is used throughout the country, including Rimini, for all financial transactions.

System Of Government

Rimini is a city in Italy. Italy has a parliamentary republic system of government. The country is governed by a combination of the President, who is the head of state, and the Prime Minister, who is the head of government.

The President of Italy is elected by an electoral college consisting of the members of the Parliament of Italy, along with regional representatives. The President's role is largely ceremonial and symbolic, representing the unity of the country.

The Prime Minister, on the other hand, is appointed by the President and is usually the leader of the political party or coalition that has the majority in the Parliament. The Prime Minister is responsible for the day-to-day administration of the government and the implementation of policies.

Rimini, being a city within Italy, falls under the overall governance of the Italian government. However, it is important to note that regional governments in Italy, such as the regional councils, also have a certain degree of administrative and legislative powers. These regional governments are responsible for issues specific to their respective regions, including some aspects of local governance.

Brief History Of Rimini

Rimini has a rich history that dates back to ancient times and has witnessed the influence of various civilizations throughout the centuries. Here is a brief overview of the history of Rimini:

Ancient Times

The area of Rimini has been inhabited since prehistoric times, as evidenced by archaeological finds. In the 3rd century BCE, it became a Roman colony known as Ariminum. Rimini served as an important hub on the Via Flaminia, a major Roman road that connected Rome to the Adriatic Sea.

Middle Ages:

During the early Middle Ages, Rimini came under the rule of various Germanic tribes, including the Ostrogoths and the Lombards. In the 9th century, it became part of the Papal States. The city faced frequent attacks and sieges, including invasions by the Byzantines, Normans, and other regional powers.

Renaissance and Modern Era

In the 15th century, Rimini came under the control of the Malatesta family, who transformed the city into a center of art and culture. Sigismondo Pandolfo Malatesta, a prominent member of the family, commissioned famous architects and artists, including Leon Battista Alberti and Piero della Francesca, to create magnificent buildings and artwork.

In the following centuries, Rimini saw a series of political changes. It came under the rule of the Papal States, the French, and then the Austrians. In the 19th century, the city became part of the unified Kingdom of Italy.

World War II and Modern Developments

During World War II, Rimini suffered heavy damage due to bombings and battles between Allied and German forces. After the war, the city went through a period of reconstruction and redevelopment. Today, Rimini is known for its beautiful beaches, historic sites, and vibrant tourism industry.

Tourism

Rimini has become a popular tourist destination, especially during the summer months. Its long sandy beaches and lively entertainment venues attract visitors from Italy and around the world. The city also hosts various trade fairs and conferences throughout the year, further contributing to its economic significance.

Rimini's historical center, known as the Borgo San Giuliano, still preserves its medieval charm with narrow streets, colorful houses, and traditional restaurants. The city is also home to several notable landmarks, including the Arch of Augustus, the Tiberius Bridge, and the Malatesta Temple.

Overall, Rimini's history is a tale of ancient origins, medieval struggles, Renaissance splendor, and modern tourism. It continues to be a vibrant and cultural city, offering a blend of historical significance and contemporary attractions.

Why Visit Rimini

There are several reasons why you should consider visiting Rimini. Here are some of the key attractions and experiences that make Rimini a worthwhile destination:

1. Beautiful Beaches
Rimini boasts stunning sandy beaches along the Adriatic Sea, making it an ideal destination for sunbathing, swimming, and water sports. The beaches are well-equipped with facilities, including beach clubs, restaurants, and water sports rentals.

2. Rich History and Architecture
Rimini has a fascinating historical heritage with well-preserved architectural landmarks. You can explore the ancient Roman ruins, such as the Arch of Augustus and the Tiberius Bridge. The Malatesta Temple, a masterpiece of Renaissance architecture, is also worth visiting.

3. Cultural Festivals
Rimini hosts numerous cultural events and festivals throughout the year. You might have the opportunity to attend events like the Rimini Meeting, an international cultural and religious gathering, or the Rimini Jazz Festival, which showcases world-class jazz performances.

4. Gastronomic Delights

Emilia-Romagna, the region where Rimini is located, is known for its exceptional cuisine. You can indulge in authentic Italian dishes like piadina, tagliatelle al ragù, and local seafood specialties. Rimini offers a wide range of restaurants, trattorias, and gelaterias to satisfy your culinary cravings.

5. Vibrant Nightlife
Rimini is renowned for its lively nightlife scene. The city comes alive after dark with numerous bars, clubs, and beachfront parties. Whether you're looking for a casual drink by the beach or an energetic night of dancing, Rimini offers a diverse range of entertainment options.

6. Nearby Attractions
Rimini's central location allows for convenient access to other popular destinations in northern Italy. You can easily take day trips to explore nearby cities like Bologna, Ravenna, and San Marino, each offering its own unique attractions and experiences.

7. Family-Friendly Atmosphere
Rimini is a family-friendly destination with several amusement parks, water parks, and activities suitable for children. Fiabilandia and Italia in Miniatura are two popular attractions that offer entertainment and educational experiences for kids of all ages.

In summary, visiting Rimini offers a combination of beautiful beaches, rich history, cultural events, delicious cuisine, vibrant nightlife, and the opportunity to explore other nearby attractions. Whether you're seeking relaxation, cultural immersion, or a fun-filled vacation, Rimini has something to offer for everyone.

CHAPTER 2

ESSENTIALS FOR YOUR TRIP TO RIMINI

Have you decided on taking that trip to Rimini? If you are serious about that awesome experience, solo, with friends or family, then read on because here in this chapter, we will delve into everything you will need to know, do and put in place for a stress free trip.

Ideal Time To Visit Rimini

To make the most of your visit to Rimini, it is essential to choose the ideal time to explore this enchanting destination. Whether you seek sun-soaked beach days or cultural immersion, understanding Rimini's seasonal variations will help you plan an unforgettable trip. Here, we present a detailed guide to the ideal time to visit Rimini, considering factors such as weather, crowd levels, and local events.

Summer (June to August)

Summer is undoubtedly the most popular time to visit Rimini, attracting sun-seekers from around the world. The weather is pleasantly warm, with temperatures ranging from 25°C to 30°C (77°F to 86°F). The sea is perfect for swimming, and the beaches come alive with vibrant beach clubs, umbrellas, and sun loungers. However, do note that this is also the peak tourist season, so the city tends to be crowded, especially in July and August. It is advisable to book accommodations well in advance during this period. Summer is also an excellent time to enjoy Rimini's lively nightlife, with various clubs and bars hosting parties and events.

Spring (March to May)

Spring offers a delightful time to visit Rimini, as the weather begins to warm up, and the crowds are relatively thinner compared to summer. Temperatures range from 15°C to 20°C (59°F to 68°F), making it pleasant for outdoor activities and sightseeing. Spring also brings colorful blossoms, adding to the city's charm. April and May are particularly suitable for exploring Rimini's historical attractions, such as the Arch of Augustus and the Tempio Malatestiano, without the summer tourist rush. Additionally, if you visit during Easter, you can experience the unique Italian traditions and festivities celebrated in Rimini.

Autumn (September to November)

Autumn in Rimini is characterized by milder temperatures, ranging from 15°C to 25°C (59°F to 77°F), making it another excellent time to explore the city. The beaches are less crowded, offering a peaceful retreat, and the sea remains warm for swimming until late

September. September is particularly ideal for those who enjoy warm weather but prefer to avoid the summer crowds. Autumn is also the harvest season, and you can savor local produce and regional delicacies at food festivals in Rimini and the surrounding countryside.

Winter (December to February)

Although Rimini is not known as a winter destination, visiting during this time offers a unique experience for travelers seeking a quieter and more authentic side of the city. The weather is cool, with temperatures ranging from 5°C to 12°C (41°F to 54°F), and it occasionally snows, creating a picturesque setting. Winter allows you to explore Rimini's historical sites, museums, and local markets without the tourist crowds. It is worth mentioning that some hotels and attractions might have reduced hours or be closed during this season, so it's advisable to check beforehand. If you are interested in local traditions, Rimini celebrates Carnival in February, offering colorful parades and festivities.

For Budget-conscious Visitors

The best seasons to visit Rimini would be spring (March to May) and autumn (September to November). Here's why:

Spring (March to May)

During spring, Rimini offers favorable weather with milder temperatures, ranging from 15°C to 20°C (59°F to 68°F). The tourist crowds are not as significant as during the summer months, resulting in lower accommodation prices and better availability. You can take advantage of discounted rates on hotels, flights, and other travel services. Additionally, with the arrival of spring, you can explore Rimini's historical landmarks, such as the Arch of Augustus and the Tempio Malatestiano, at your own pace, without the rush of peak tourist season.

Autumn (September to November)

Autumn in Rimini offers similar advantages for budget travelers. The weather remains pleasant, with temperatures ranging from 15°C to 25°C (59°F to 77°F), making it an ideal time for outdoor activities and sightseeing. As the summer crowds disperse, you can find more affordable accommodation options and enjoy lower prices for various services. September, in particular, provides a balance between warm weather and reduced tourist activity, allowing you to enjoy the beaches and attractions without the peak season prices.

In both seasons, you may also find discounts and special offers at local restaurants, as well as at regional food festivals where you can savor local cuisine and delicacies without breaking the bank.

Overall, by planning your visit to Rimini during the spring or autumn seasons, you can enjoy favorable weather, fewer crowds, and potentially lower costs for accommodations, transportation, and activities, making it an ideal choice for budget-conscious travelers.

Visas And Documents Requirements (If Visiting From Outside Italy)

If you are visiting Rimini, Italy from outside the country, you will need to ensure that you have the necessary visas and documents to enter and stay in Italy. The specific requirements may vary depending on your nationality and the purpose and duration of your visit. However, we can provide you with a general overview of the visa and document requirements for visiting Rimini as a tourist. It's always recommended to check the latest updates from the official Italian embassy or consulate in your country before traveling.

Visa Requirements

- Check if you require a visa: Determine if you need a visa to enter Italy by checking the official website of the Italian Ministry of Foreign Affairs or contacting the nearest Italian embassy or consulate in your country.

Tourist Visa (Schengen Visa)

A tourist visa, also known as a Schengen visa, allows you to visit Italy and other countries in the Schengen Area for tourism, sightseeing, and leisure activities.

The Schengen Area comprises 26 European countries that have abolished passport control at their mutual borders, allowing for easy movement within the area.

With a Schengen visa, you can stay in Italy for a maximum of 90 days within a 180-day period.

The visa is generally issued for single or multiple entries, depending on your specific circumstances and the duration of your trip.

To apply for a tourist visa, you will need to submit the required documents, including a completed visa application form, a valid passport, travel insurance, proof of accommodation in Italy, proof of sufficient funds, and a return ticket or proof of onward travel.

It's important to apply for the visa in advance at the Italian embassy or consulate in your country of residence. The application process usually involves submitting the required documents, paying the visa fee, and attending an interview if necessary.

The processing time for a tourist visa can vary, so it's advisable to apply well in advance of your intended travel dates.

Once you have obtained the Schengen visa, you can travel to Rimini and explore other parts of Italy within the allowed duration.

Remember to check the official website of the Italian Ministry of Foreign Affairs or contact the Italian embassy or consulate in your country for the most accurate and up-to-date information regarding the tourist visa application process and requirements specific to your nationality.

Other Visa Types

In addition to the tourist visa (Schengen visa) mentioned earlier, there are other visa options available depending on the purpose and duration of your visit to Rimini or Italy. Here are a few common types of Visa:

Work Visa

If you are planning to work in Rimini or Italy, you will need to apply for a work visa. The specific type of work visa will depend on factors such as the nature of your work, duration of employment, and your qualifications.

You will typically need a job offer or sponsorship from an Italian employer to apply for a work visa.

Student Visa

If you plan to study in Rimini or Italy, you will need to apply for a student visa. You will generally require an acceptance letter from an Italian educational institution, proof of financial means to support your studies, and sometimes proof of health insurance coverage.

Business Visa

If you are visiting Rimini for business purposes, such as attending conferences, meetings, or negotiations, you may need to apply for a business visa. It allows for short-term business activities in Italy, but it does not permit employment.

Family Reunification Visa

If you have family members who are Italian citizens or legal residents in Italy, you may be eligible for a family reunification visa. This type of visa allows you to join your family in Italy and stay for an extended period, subject to certain requirements.

Study Abroad or Exchange Program Visa

If you are participating in a study abroad or exchange program in Rimini or Italy, your educational institution may provide guidance on the specific visa requirements. These programs often have specific visa categories tailored to students participating in academic exchanges.

Long-Term Visa or Residence Permit

If you plan to stay in Italy for an extended period, beyond the allowed duration of a tourist visa, you may need to apply for a long-term visa or residence permit. This applies to purposes such as work, study, family reunification, or other specific circumstances.

It's important to note that each visa type has its own specific requirements, application procedures, and processing times. It's recommended to consult the official website of the Italian Ministry of Foreign Affairs or contact the nearest Italian embassy or consulate in your country to obtain the most accurate and up-to-date information regarding the visa options that are applicable to your situation.

Valid Passport

You have to ensure that your passport is valid for at least six months beyond your intended stay duration in Italy. It should also have like two blank pages at least for visa stamps.

Travel Insurance

It is highly recommended to have travel insurance that covers medical expenses, emergency evacuation, and repatriation for the duration of your stay in Italy. Some insurance policies also include trip cancellation or interruption coverage.

Proof of Accommodation

Provide proof of your accommodation in Rimini, such as hotel reservations, a letter of invitation from a host, or any other document confirming your place of stay.

Proof of Sufficient Funds

You may be asked to provide evidence of sufficient financial means (like bank statements, credit card statements etc) to support yourself during your stay in Italy.

Return Ticket

It is generally required to have a confirmed return ticket or proof of onward travel to your home country or another destination outside the Schengen Area.

Additional Documents

Depending on your circumstances, you may be asked to provide additional documents such as a travel itinerary, proof of employment, proof of educational enrollment, or a letter explaining the purpose of your visit.

Remember, the specific requirements can vary, so it's important to consult the official Italian embassy or consulate in your country for the most accurate and up-to-date information regarding visas and documents for visiting Rimini or any other part of Italy.

What To Pack For Your Trip To Rimini

When packing for your trip to Rimini, Italy, consider the following items:

Clothing

Lightweight and comfortable clothes suitable for warm weather, as Rimini has a Mediterranean climate.

T-shirts, light trousers, skirts, dresses, and shorts.

Swimsuits or beachwear if you plan to enjoy the beaches.

A light jacket or sweater for cooler weather in the evenings.

Footwear

Comfortable walking shoes, boots or sandals for exploring the city's attractions.

Flip-flops for the sandy beaches.

A pair of dressier shoes if you plan to visit upscale restaurants or clubs.

Accessories

Sun Hat or cap to protect yourself from the sun.

Sunglasses to protect your eyes from the harsh sunlight.

A small umbrella in case it starts to rain unexpectedly.

A beach towel for sunbathing or lounging on the sand.

Toiletries

Travel-sized toiletries, including shampoo, conditioner, soap, and toothpaste.

Good Sunscreen to protect your skin from the sun.

Insect repellent.

Electronics

Adapters or converters for electrical outlets if you're traveling from a country with different plug types.

Your mobile phone, camera, or any other electronic devices you may need.

Chargers and extra batteries and other accessories for your electronic devices.

Miscellaneous Items

Travel documents, including your passport, ID, travel insurance, and any required visas.

A copy of your hotel reservations and contact information.

Money, credit cards, and some local currency (Euros).

A reusable water bottle to always keep yourself hydrated.

Remember to pack according to the season and activities you plan to engage in during your trip. It's also a good idea to check the weather forecast closer to your travel date to ensure you have appropriate clothing and gear.

Getting To Rimini

To reach Rimini, Italy, you have several transportation options depending on your starting location. Here are your options of travel:

By Plane

If you are coming from a distant location or another country, flying to Rimini is often the most convenient option. The closest airport is Federico Fellini International Airport (RMI), located in Miramare, just a few kilometers away from Rimini city center. Several airlines operate flights to Rimini from various European cities. Once you arrive at the airport, you can take a taxi, bus, or train to reach your final destination within Rimini.

By Train

Rimini is well-connected to major Italian cities through an extensive railway network. You can take a train from cities like Rome, Florence, Milan, Bologna, Venice, or Naples, among others. The Rimini train station is centrally located and easily accessible. It is advisable to check the train schedules and book your tickets in advance, especially during peak travel seasons.

Train From Outside Italy

Rimini is also connected to the international rail network, making it accessible by train from various European cities. You can check train connections to Rimini from neighboring countries such as Switzerland, Austria, Germany, France, and Slovenia. Major cities like Zurich, Vienna, Munich, Paris, and Ljubljana have direct train services to Rimini or connections with transfers. It's recommended to check the train schedules and book your tickets in advance, as international train journeys may require reservations.

By Bus

Buses are another option to consider, particularly if you are traveling from nearby cities or towns. Rimini has a reliable bus network, and several companies provide intercity bus services to and from Rimini. You can check the bus schedules and book tickets online or at the bus station in your departure city.

Bus From Outside Italy

Bus travel is another option to consider when traveling to Rimini from outside Italy. Some long-distance bus companies operate routes connecting Rimini to different European cities. Companies like FlixBus, Eurolines, or Baltour provide international bus services to Rimini from countries such as Switzerland, Austria, Germany, France, and Slovenia. These bus journeys often involve multiple stops and transfers, so it's important to check the schedules, routes, and availability in advance.

When planning your trip, make sure to check the specific transportation options available from your starting location and consult the websites or contact the respective train or bus operators for up-to-date information on routes, schedules, and ticket bookings.

By Car

If you prefer driving, you can reach Rimini by car. Italy has an extensive highway network, and Rimini is well-connected to the national road system. You can use a GPS or map application to plan your route. However, keep in mind that parking in the city center can be limited and expensive, so it's advisable to check for parking options in advance.

Once you arrive in Rimini, you can explore the city's attractions, such as its beautiful beaches, historic landmarks, and vibrant nightlife. Additionally, Rimini serves as a gateway to other popular destinations in the region, including San Marino, Ravenna, and the nearby coastal towns along the Adriatic Sea.

By Boat

While Rimini is actually a coastal city located on the Adriatic Sea in the Emilia-Romagna region of Italy. It is known for its long sandy beaches and vibrant tourism industry. Reaching Rimini directly by boat is not a common mode of transportation, as Rimini is not a major seaport. However, there are alternative options if you are interested in incorporating a boat journey into your travel itinerary:

Ferries to nearby ports

Rimini is located on the Adriatic coast of Italy, and there are ferry services available to nearby ports along the Adriatic Sea. For example, you can consider taking a ferry to Ancona, which is a larger port city located approximately 90 kilometers north of Rimini. From Ancona, you can then continue your journey to Rimini by train or bus.

Cruises

Some cruise ships include Rimini as a port of call during their Mediterranean itineraries. These cruises typically depart from larger ports in countries such as Italy, Greece, or Croatia. While this option allows you to visit Rimini as part of a larger cruise experience, it may not provide a direct route or extensive time to explore the city.

If you are considering traveling to Rimini by boat, it is important to research available ferry routes, schedules, and companies that serve the Adriatic region. Keep in mind that ferry services may have limited availability depending on the season, and it's advisable to plan your journey well in advance to ensure smooth connections with other modes of transportation.

Getting Around Rimini

Getting around Rimini is relatively easy due to its efficient public transportation system and compact size. Here are some common methods of transportation for getting around Rimini:

Bus

Rimini has a well-developed bus network that covers the city and its surrounding areas. The local bus company, Trasporto Passeggeri Emilia-Romagna (TPER), operates numerous routes throughout the city. Buses are an affordable and convenient way to travel within Rimini, and they generally run from early morning until late evening. You can purchase tickets directly from the driver or at designated ticket counters.

Train

Rimini's train station, Rimini Centrale, is centrally located and serves as a transportation hub connecting the city with other destinations in Italy. If you plan to explore nearby towns or cities, taking a train can be a convenient option. The train services are operated by Trenitalia and offer connections to major Italian cities like Bologna, Florence, Venice, and Rome.

Bicycle

Rimini is a bicycle-friendly city, and cycling is a popular means of transportation. You can rent bicycles from various rental shops or use the Rimini Bike Sharing service, which provides bicycles for short-term use. The city has dedicated bike lanes and paths, making it easy to navigate and explore the area on two wheels.

Walking

Rimini's city center is compact and easily walkable, allowing you to explore many attractions on foot. The historical center, with its narrow streets and ancient architecture, is particularly enjoyable to explore by walking. Most of the main landmarks, shops, restaurants, and entertainment venues are within walking distance of each other.

Taxi

Taxis are available in Rimini, and you can find them at designated taxi stands or book one through taxi companies. Taxis can be a convenient option for shorter journeys or when you have heavy luggage. It's recommended to confirm the fare with the driver before the ride or ask for a metered fare.

It's worth noting that Rimini is a popular tourist destination, and during peak travel seasons, such as the summer months, public transportation can be busier than usual. Therefore, it's a good idea to plan your transportation in advance, especially if you have specific schedules or destinations in mind.

What About Ride Sharing Services?

Ride-sharing services such as Uber and Lyft are not widely available in Rimini. These services are more commonly found in larger cities or metropolitan areas. However, in Rimini, you can consider using local ride-hailing or taxi apps, which provide similar services:

MyTaxi
MyTaxi is a popular ride-hailing app in Italy that allows you to book a taxi conveniently from your smartphone. It provides information about the estimated fare, driver details, and the ability to track your ride. You can download the MyTaxi app and use it to book a taxi in Rimini.

NCC (Noleggio con Conducente)
NCC services are private chauffeur services available in Italy. These services provide luxury cars and professional drivers for transportation. You can pre-book an NCC service through various companies or apps, specifying your pickup location, destination, and desired time.

When using ride-hailing or taxi apps, it's important to have a stable internet connection and a compatible smartphone. Additionally, it's advisable to check the availability and pricing of these services in Rimini, as it may vary depending on the season and demand.

Alternatively, traditional taxi services are widely available in Rimini. You can find taxis at designated taxi stands or by calling a local taxi company:

+39 366 132 9141 (NCC Rimini)
+39 349 387 6246 (NCC Rimini)
+39 054 150 020 (Radio Taxi Rimini)

It's recommended to confirm the fare with the driver before starting the journey or ask for a metered fare.

As the availability of ride-sharing services can change over time, it's always a good idea to check for the latest updates and options available in Rimini during your travel dates.

Accommodations In Rimini (Where To Stay In Rimini)

Rimini offers a wide range of Accommodations options to accommodate different budgets and preferences. Here are a few popular options:

Hotels And Resorts

1. Grand Hotel Rimini
Located on the seafront, this historic 5-star hotel offers luxurious accommodation with elegant rooms, a private beach, a swimming pool, and

multiple dining options. It is known for its classic architecture and excellent service.

Address: Parco fellini1, Rimini Central Marina, 47900 Rimini, Italy (about 1.0 miles from center).

Contact Info: +39 0541 56000

Beaches Nearby
- Rimini Prime Beach (about 450 ft away from property.
- Lido San Giuliano Beach (about 2050 ft away from property)
- Viserbella Beach (about 0.7 mi away from property)

2. Hotel Sporting
Situated in the heart of Rimini's Marina Centro area, Hotel Sporting is a 4-star hotel offering comfortable rooms, a rooftop swimming pool, a wellness center, and direct beach access. It is a popular choice for both leisure and business travelers.

Address: Viale Vespucci 20, Rimini Central Marina 47921 Rimini, Italy (about 0.8 miles from center).

Contact Info: +39 0541 55391

Beaches Nearby

- Rimini Prime Beach (about 250 ft away from property.
- Lido San Giuliano Beach (about 0.7 mi away from property)
- Viserbella Beach (about 1 mi away from property)
- Rimini Dog Beach (about 1.6 mi away from property)

3. Parco dei Principi Boutique Hotel

This 4-star hotel is located near the beach and features modern rooms, a rooftop swimming pool, a restaurant, and a fitness center. It offers a peaceful atmosphere and is suitable for families and couples.

Address: Viale Regina Elena 98, Rimini Central Marina, 47900 Rimini, Italy (about 1.5 miles from center).

Contact Info: +39 0833 543000

Beaches Nearby
- Rimini Prime Beach (about 250 ft away from property)
- Rimini Dog Beach (about 550 ft away from property)
- Libera Beach (about 2350 ft away from property)
- Pradipo Beach (about 0.9 mi away from property)

- Miramare Beach (about 1.5 mi away from property)

4. Hotel Ambasciatori
Situated on the seafront promenade, Hotel Ambasciatori is a 4-star hotel offering comfortable rooms, a private beach area, a rooftop swimming pool, and a wellness center. It is known for its attentive staff and convenient location.

Address: Viale Vespucci 22, Rimini Central Marina, 47921 Rimini, Italy (about 0.8 miles from center).

Contact Info: +39 0541 148 1204

Beaches Nearby
- Rimini Prime Beach (about 300 ft away from property)
- Lido San Giuliano Beach (about 0.7 mi away from property)
- Viserbella Beach (about 1 mi away from property)
- Rimini Dog Beach (about 1.6 mi away from property)

5. Hotel Diplomat Palace
Located near Rimini's historic center, Hotel Diplomat Palace is a 4-star hotel offering spacious rooms, a rooftop swimming pool, a

restaurant, and a fitness center. It provides easy access to both the beach and the city's attractions.

Address: Viale Regina Elena 70, Rimini Central Marina, 47900 Rimini, Italy (about 1.3 miles from center).

Contact Info: +39 0541 380011

Beaches Nearby
- Rimini Prime Beach (about 160 ft away from property)
- Rimini Dog Beach (about 2150 ft away from property)
- Libera Beach (about 0.8 mi away from property)
- Bradipo Beach (about 1.2 mi away from property)
- Miramare Beach (about 1.8 mi away from property)

6. Savoia Hotel Rimini
Situated on the seafront, Hotel Savoia is a 4-star hotel offering comfortable rooms, a swimming pool, a restaurant, and a terrace overlooking the sea.

Address: Lungomare Murri 13, Rimini Central Marina, 47900 Rimini Italy (about 0.8 miles from center).

Contact Info: +39 0541 396600

Beaches Nearby
- Rimini Prime Beach (about 160 ft away from property)
- Lido San Giuliano Beach (about 1 mi away from property)
- Rimini Dog Beach (1.3 mi away from property)
- Viserbella Beach (1.3 mi away from property)
- Libera Beach (1.6 mi away from property)

7. Card International Hotel

Located in Rimini's historic center, Hotel Card International is a boutique hotel offering stylish rooms, a rooftop terrace with panoramic views, a wellness center, and a restaurant. It is known for its contemporary design and central location.

Address: Via Dante Alighieri 50, Rimini Centro, 47900 Rimini, Italy (about 1000 ft from city center).

Contact Info: +39 0541 26412

Beaches Nearby
- Rimini Prime Beach (0.7 mi away from property)

- Lido San Giuliano Beach (about 1 mi away from property)
- Viserbella Beach (about 1.1 mi away from property)
- Rimini Dog Beach (about 1.6 mi away from property)

8. Hotel Milton Rimini

Situated on the seafront, Hotel Milton Rimini is a 4-star hotel offering comfortable rooms, a private beach area, an outdoor swimming pool, and a restaurant. It is popular for its family-friendly atmosphere and entertainment activities.

Address: Via Cappellini 1/A, Rimini Central Marina, 47921 Rimini, Italy (about 1.0 miles from center)

Contact Info: +39 0541 54600

Beaches Nearby
- Rimini Prime Beach (about 350 ft away from property)
- Lido San Giuliano Beach (about 1900 ft away from property)
- Viserbella Beach (about 0.7 mi away from property)

9. Hotel De Londres: This 4-star hotel is located on Rimini's seafront and features modern rooms, a rooftop terrace with a panoramic pool, a spa

center, and a restaurant. It offers stunning sea views and a relaxing ambiance.

Address: Viale Amerigo Vespucci, 24, Rimini Central Marina, 47921 Rimini, Italy (about 0.8 miles from center)

Contact Info: +39 0541 50114

Beaches Nearby
- Rimini Prime Beach (about 300 ft away from property)
- Lido San Giuliano Beach (about 0.7 mi away from property)
- Viserbella Beach (about 1 mi away from property)
- Rimini Dog Beach (about 1.6 mi away from property)

10. Hotel Bellevue
Situated in the Miramare area of Rimini, Hotel Bellevue is a 3-star hotel offering comfortable rooms, a swimming pool, a restaurant, and a bar. It is known for its warm hospitality and proximity to the beach.

Address: Piazzale John Fitzgerald Kennedy 12, Rimini Central Marina, 47900 Rimini, Italy (about 0.8 miles from center)

Contact Info: +39 0541 390490

Beaches Nearby
- Rimini Prime Beach (about 200 ft away from property)
- Lido San Giuliano Beach (about 0.9 mi away from property)
- Viserbella Beach (about 1.2 mi away from property)
- Rimini Dog Beach (about 1.4 mi away from property)
- Libera Beach (about 1.8 mi away from property)

11. Hotel Derby

Situated near Rimini's historic center, Hotel Derby is a budget-friendly option offering comfortable rooms, a restaurant, and a bar. It provides easy access to the city's attractions and is suitable for travelers on a tighter budget.

Address: Viale Regina Elena, 88/A, Rimini Central Marina, 47921 Rimini, Italy (about 1.5 miles from center)

Contact Info: +39 0541 380724

Beaches Nearby
- Rimini Prime Beach (about 160 ft away from property)
- Rimini Dog Beach (about 950 ft away from property)

- Libera Beach (about 2800 ft away from property)
- Pradipo Beach (about 1 mi away from property)
- Miramare Beach (about 1.6 mi away from property)

Remember to consider your specific needs, such as location, amenities, and budget, when choosing a hotel or resort in Rimini. It's also recommended to check the latest availability, rates, and customer reviews before making a reservation. **Booking.com** or **Tripadvisor.com** could help with accommodation bookings.

Bed And Breakfasts

Rimini also offers a variety of charming bed and breakfast accommodations for travelers seeking a more intimate and cozy stay. Here are some bed and breakfast options in Rimini:

1. Villa Azzurra
Located in the heart of Rimini, Villa Azzurra is a bed and breakfast offering comfortable rooms with a traditional Italian ambiance. It features a garden, a terrace, and a communal lounge area. It is known for its warm hospitality and homemade breakfast.

Address: Viale Pegli, 17, 47924 Rimini RN, Italy (about 2.6 miles from center)

Contact Info: +39 0541 378828

Beaches Nearby
- Bradipo Beach (about 850 ft away from property)
- Libera Beach (about 1700 ft away from property)
- Miramare Beach (about 1850 ft away from property)
- Rimini Dog Beach (about 0.7 mi away from property)
- Rimini Prime Beach (about 1.1 mi away from property)
- Riccione Beach (about 1.4 mi away from property)

2. Villa Maldestra
The villa is nestled in a serene setting, surrounded by lush greenery, and offers a glimpse into the grandeur of a bygone era.

Address: 17 Viale Umago, San Giuliano, 47921 Rimini, Italy (about 0.6 miles from center)

Contact: +39 331 437 0161

Beaches Nearby

- Viserbella Beach (about 0.7 mi away from property)
- Lido San Giuliano Beach(about 0.7 mi away from property)
- Rimini Prime Beach (about 1.1 mi away from property)

3. Angolo Relax Camera King

This property offers comfort, relaxation and noise free environment, plus breakfast of course.
Address: 12 Piazzale Cesare Battisti, Rimini Central Marina, 47921 Rimini, Italy (about 500 feet from center)

Contact Info: +39 380 156 5894

Beaches Nearby

- Rimini Prime Beach (about 2950 ft away from property)
- Lido San Giuliano Beach (about 0.8 mi away from property)
- Viserbella Beach (about 1 mi away from property)
- Rimini Dog Beach (about 1.6 mi away from property)

4. Hotel Blue Sky

This property offers a range of room options to suit different preferences and group sizes. These may include single, double, triple, and family rooms. The rooms are designed with a focus on comfort and may feature amenities such as en-suite bathrooms, air conditioning, flat-screen TVs, and complimentary Wi-Fi.

Address: Viale Viareggio, 14 Rivazzura, Rivazzurra, Rimini, Italy (about 2.8 miles from center)

Contact Info: +39 328 117 8348

Beaches Nearby
- Bradipo Beach (about 1000 ft away from property)
- Miramare Beach (about 1150 ft away from property)
- Libera Beach (about 2750 ft away from property)
- Rimini Dog Beach (about 0.9 mi away from property)
- Riccione Beach (about 1.2 mi away from property)
- Rimini Prime Beach (about 1.3 mi away from property)

5. Villa La Torretta Luxury B&B
Villa La Torretta Luxury B&B is a prestigious and upscale bed and breakfast located in Rimini, Italy. It offers a luxurious and intimate setting for guests seeking a refined and elegant stay. Here is an overview of Villa La Torretta Luxury B&B:

Address: 117 Viale Giuliano Dati, Viserba, Rimini Italy (about 2.8 miles from center)

Contact Info: +39 0541 380286

Beaches Nearby
- Viserbella Beach (about 160 ft away from property)
- Marina Di Viserbella Beach (about 160 ft away from property)
- Torre Pedrera Beach (about 0.8 mi away from property)
- Lido San Giuliano Beach (about 1.8 mi away from property)

6. Sottoalfico B&B

Sottoalfico B&B Rimini offers a charming and intimate accommodation option for travelers seeking a cozy and authentic experience. With its comfortable rooms, friendly hosts, delightful breakfast, and convenient location, it provides a homely retreat in the beautiful city of Rimini.

Address: Via dell'Abetone 2, Rimini, Italy (about 2.0 miles from center)

Contact Info: +39 338 161 5198

7. Hotel Half Moon

This property is known for its warm and welcoming hospitality. The hosts are typically friendly, attentive, and eager to assist guests with their needs. They may provide personalized recommendations for local attractions, restaurants, and activities, ensuring that guests make the most of their stay in Rimini.

Address: 18 Viale Brindisi, Rivazzurra, Rimini, Italy (about 2.5 miles from center)

Contact Info: +39 329 161 8976

Beaches Nearby
- Bradipo Beach (about 800 ft away from property)
- Libera Beach (about 1100 ft away from property)
- Miramare Beach (about 2500 ft away from property)
- Rimini Dog Beach (about 3150 ft away from property)
- Rimini Prime Beach (about 1 mi away from property)
- Riccione Beach (about 1.5 mi away from property)

Remember to check the specific details, availability, and customer reviews of each establishment when making your selection.

Vacation Rentals And Apartments

Rimini offers a variety of vacation rentals and apartments that provide a more independent and spacious accommodation option for travelers. Here are some resources and platforms where you can find vacation rentals and apartments in Rimini:

1. Airbnb (www.airbnb.com)
Airbnb is a popular online platform that allows individuals to rent out their homes, apartments, or rooms to travelers. You can search for vacation rentals and apartments in Rimini on Airbnb, filtering based on your preferred dates, amenities, and budget.

2. Booking.com (www.booking.com)
Booking.com is a well-known online travel agency that offers a wide range of accommodation options, including vacation rentals and apartments. You can search for apartments in Rimini on their website, specifying your travel dates and preferences.

3. HomeAway (www.homeaway.com)
HomeAway is a vacation rental marketplace where you can find a selection of apartments and vacation homes in Rimini. You can browse through their listings, filter based on your requirements, and directly contact the property owners or managers.

4. VRBO (www.vrbo.com)
VRBO (Vacation Rentals by Owner) is another platform that connects travelers with vacation rental properties. You can search for apartments and vacation homes in Rimini on VRBO, view property details, and make bookings directly with the property owners.

When searching for vacation rentals and apartments, it's essential to review the property details, guest reviews, and cancellation policies. Be sure to communicate with the hosts or property owners to clarify any questions you may have before making a reservation.

Additionally, it's advisable to book your vacation rental or apartment well in advance, especially during peak travel seasons, to secure the best options and availability.

Budget And Hostel Options

Rimini also offers budget-friendly accommodation options, including hostels and budget hotels, for travelers looking to minimize their expenses. Here are some budget and hostel options in Rimini:

1. Sunflower Beach Backpacker Hostel
Located near the beach in Rimini's Rivazzurra neighborhood, Sunflower Beach Backpacker Hostel is a popular choice among budget travelers. It offers dormitory-style rooms with

shared bathrooms, a communal kitchen, a bar, and a lively social atmosphere.

Address: Via Siracusa 25, Marebello, Rimini, Italy (2.1 miles away from property)

Contact Info: +39 0541 373432

2. Hotel Memory
Situated in the Marina Centro area, Hotel Memory is a budget hotel offering comfortable rooms at affordable rates. It provides a bar, a terrace, and a 24-hour front desk. The hotel is known for its convenient location and friendly staff.

Address: Viale Zanzur 7, Rimini Central Marina, Rimini, Italy (about 1.7 miles from center)

Contact Info: +39 0541 391230

3. Hotel Boom
Located in Rimini's Viserbella neighborhood, Hotel Boom is a budget hotel offering simple and clean rooms. It features a restaurant, a bar, and a shared lounge area. The hotel is known for its value for money and proximity to the beach.

Address: Via Podgora 5, Rivabella, Rimini, Italy (about 1.3 miles from center)

Contact Info: +39 328 257 1284

4. Hotel River fronte Mare Con Piscina
Situated near Rimini's train station, Hotel River offers affordable rooms with basic amenities. It features a bar, a terrace, and a 24-hour front desk. The hotel provides easy access to public transportation and is a good option for budget-conscious travelers.

Address: Via Ortigara 21, San Giuliano, Rimini, Italy (about 1.1 miles from center)

Contact Info: +39 0541 26904

5. Hotel Pigalle
Located in the Marina Centro area, Hotel Pigalle is a budget-friendly hotel offering compact rooms with essential amenities. It features a bar, a terrace, and a 24-hour front desk. The hotel is known for its central location and competitive prices.

Address: Via Ugo Foscolo 7, Rimini Central Marina, Rimini Italy (about 0.8 miles from center)

Contact Info: +39 0541 391054

6. Hotel Bianca Vela
located in Rimini's Bellariva area, Hotel Bianca Vela is a budget hotel offering comfortable rooms

at reasonable prices. It features a restaurant, a bar, and a shared lounge area. The hotel is known for its value for money and friendly atmosphere.

Address: Via Adria 9, Rimini Miramare, Rimini, Italy (about 3.3 miles from center)

Contact Info: +39 0541 183 5568

7. Hotel Alibi

Situated near Rimini's historic center, Hotel Alibi is a budget-friendly hotel offering basic rooms with essential amenities. It features a bar, a terrace, and a 24-hour front desk. The hotel provides easy access to the city's attractions and public transportation.

Address: Viale Bengasi 14, Rimini Central Marina, Rimini, Italy (about 0.7 miles from center)

Contact: +39 0541 380764

8. Hotel Caraibi

Situated in the Rivazzurra neighborhood, Hotel Caraibi is a budget-friendly hotel offering comfortable rooms at competitive prices. It features a restaurant, a bar, and a shared lounge area. The hotel is known for its family-friendly atmosphere and proximity to the beach.

Address: via trapani 3, Rivazzurra, Rimini, Italy (about 2.5 miles from center)

Contact Info: +39 0541 372615

9. Hotel San Francisco Spiaggia

Located near Rimini's seafront, Hotel San Francisco Spiaggia is a budget hotel offering basic rooms with convenient amenities. It features a restaurant, a bar, and a terrace. The hotel is known for its affordable rates and proximity to the beach.

Address: Viale Regina Margherita 42, Rivazzurra, Rimini, Italy (about 2.7 miles from center)

Contact Info: +39 0541 371559

10. Jammin's Hostel & Bar Rimini

What sets Jammin's Hostel apart is its lively bar and communal spaces. The hostel features a vibrant bar area where guests can mingle, socialize, and enjoy a wide selection of drinks and cocktails. It's a fantastic place to meet fellow travelers from around the world and make new friends.

Address: Viale Derna, 22, Rimini, Italy (about 0.7 miles from center)

Contact Info: +39 0541 183 2078

These budget and hostel options provide a range of choices for travelers on a tighter budget. As always, it's advisable to check the specific details, availability, and customer reviews of each establishment before making a booking.

Unique Stays And Luxury Retreats

Rimini offers some unique and luxurious accommodations for travelers seeking a special and indulgent experience. Here are a few options for unique stays and luxury retreats in Rimini:

1. I-Suite Hotel

Situated on Rimini's seafront, I-Suite Hotel is a 5-star design hotel that offers modern and stylish suites with panoramic views of the Adriatic Sea. It features a rooftop pool, a wellness center, a private beach, and a gourmet restaurant. The hotel is known for its contemporary design and luxurious amenities.

Address: Viale Regina Elena 28, Rimini Central Marina, Rimini, Italy (about 1.0 miles from center)

Contact Info: +39 0541 309671

Beaches Nearby
- Rimini Prime Beach (about 200 ft away from property)
- Rimini Dog Beach (about 0.8 mi away from property)
- Libera Beach (about 1.2 mi away from property)
- Lido San Giuliano Beach (about 1.4 mi away from property)
- Bradipo Beach (about 1.6 mi away from property)
- Viserbella Beach (about 1.7 mi away from property)

2. Villa Adriatica
Situated in the Marina Centro area, Villa Adriatica is a boutique hotel housed in an Art Nouveau villa. It offers beautifully decorated rooms and suites, a garden, a swimming pool, and a wellness area. The hotel is known for its attention to detail and personalized service.

Address: Viale Vespucci 3, Rimini Central Marina, Rimini, Italy (about 0.9 miles from center)

Contact Info: +39 0541 54599

Beaches Nearby
- Rimini Prime Beach (about 500 ft away from property)

- Lido San Giuliano Beach (about 2850 ft away from property)
- Viserbella Beach (about 0.9 ft away from property)
- Rimini Dog Beach (about 1.7 mi away from property)

These are just a few of the unique stays and luxury retreats options in Rimini. Each offers a distinct experience and a range of luxurious amenities and services. It's advisable to check the specific details, availability, and customer reviews of each property to find the one that aligns with your preferences and desires.

CHAPTER 3

WHAT TO DO IN RIMINI

Rimini, with its vibrant atmosphere and rich history, offers a wide array of activities and attractions for visitors to enjoy. Whether you're seeking cultural experiences, beachside relaxation, or exciting nightlife, Rimini has something for everyone. In this chapter, we'll explore some of the top things to do in Rimini, highlighting its historical landmarks, cultural offerings, natural beauty, and entertainment options. Let's dive in and discover the best of Rimini!

Must See Landmarks

When exploring Rimini, there are several must-see landmarks that showcase its historical and cultural significance. Here are some of the top landmarks to visit:

1. The Arch of Augustus

As one of Rimini's most iconic symbols, the Arch of Augustus is an ancient Roman triumphal arch dating back to 27 BC. It marks the entrance to the city and serves as a testament to its Roman heritage. The arch features intricate carvings and provides a glimpse into Rimini's ancient past.

2. Tiberius Bridge
Another impressive Roman structure, the Tiberius Bridge spans the Marecchia River and dates back to the 1st century AD. This well-preserved bridge is an architectural marvel, and walking across it offers stunning views of the river and surrounding area. It's a significant historical landmark and a symbol of Rimini.

3. Tempio Malatestiano
Also known as the Malatesta Temple, this grand cathedral was designed by renowned architect Leon Battista Alberti in the 15th century. The Tempio Malatestiano features a blend of Gothic and Renaissance styles and serves as a mausoleum for the Malatesta family. Inside, you'll find beautiful frescoes and intricate details.

4. Rimini Old Town (Centro Storico)
Take a stroll through Rimini's historic center to experience its charming medieval streets and picturesque squares. Discover quaint shops, local cafés, and historical buildings as you wander through the narrow alleys. The Old Town is a treasure trove of architectural gems and a testament to Rimini's rich history.

5. Castel Sismondo
This imposing fortress was commissioned by Sigismondo Pandolfo Malatesta, a prominent ruler of Rimini, in the 15th century. Castel

Sismondo features a striking brick exterior and hosts various cultural events and exhibitions. Exploring its courtyards and towers provides a glimpse into the city's medieval past.

6. Piazza Cavour

Located in the heart of Rimini, Piazza Cavour is a vibrant square surrounded by historic buildings, lively cafés, and restaurants. It's an excellent spot for people-watching and enjoying the bustling atmosphere. The piazza is particularly enchanting in the evenings when it comes alive with locals and tourists.

7. The Surgeon's House (Domus del Chirurgo)

Located in Rimini's historic center, the Surgeon's House is an archaeological site that showcases a well-preserved Roman house. It provides a fascinating insight into daily life during Roman times, featuring intricate mosaics, frescoes, and medical instruments. Guided tours offer a deeper understanding of this ancient dwelling.

8. Rimini Roman Amphitheater

Discover the remnants of Rimini's Roman Amphitheater, located near the Arch of Augustus. Although much of it is now underground, the site offers a glimpse into the city's Roman entertainment culture. Visitors can explore the remaining structures and learn about the history of gladiatorial games and performances.

9. Malatesta Fortress (Rocca Malatestiana)
Situated in the nearby town of Verucchio, the Malatesta Fortress is a medieval castle perched on a hilltop. Built in the 12th century, it offers panoramic views of the surrounding countryside. Inside, you can explore its towers, walk along the fortified walls, and visit the museum showcasing historical artifacts.

10. Federico Fellini Museum
Rimini is the hometown of the famous Italian film director Federico Fellini. The Federico Fellini Museum is dedicated to his life and works, featuring memorabilia, photographs, and exhibits that provide insights into his creative genius. Film enthusiasts can delve into the world of this iconic filmmaker and gain a deeper appreciation for his contributions to cinema.

These landmarks offer a glimpse into Rimini's rich history and architectural beauty. They provide an opportunity to immerse yourself in the city's heritage and appreciate its cultural significance. Make sure to allocate time in your itinerary to explore these must-see landmarks and experience the historical charm of Rimini.

Iconic Museums And Galleries (In And Near Rimini)

Rimini boasts several museums and galleries that offer a diverse range of art, history, and cultural exhibits. Here are some iconic museums and galleries to explore in and near Rimini:

1. City Museum (Museo della Città)
Located in Rimini's historic center, the City Museum delves into the history and heritage of the city. It houses a collection of archaeological artifacts, artworks, and historical documents, offering insights into Rimini's past from Roman times to the present day.

2. Federico Fellini Museum
Dedicated to the renowned Italian filmmaker Federico Fellini, the museum provides a fascinating journey into his life and cinematic works. Exhibits include original sketches, costumes, photographs, and personal items that reflect Fellini's distinctive style and imaginative storytelling.

3. Museum of Contemporary Art (Museo d'Arte Moderna)
Situated in the former Pescheria Vecchia (Old Fish Market) building, the Museum of Contemporary Art showcases contemporary art

exhibitions by both Italian and international artists. The collection spans various mediums, which includes sculptures, paintings, installations, and even multimedia art.

4. Luigi Tonini Civic Museum

Housed within the ancient Malatesta Castle, the Luigi Tonini Civic Museum features a wide range of archaeological artifacts, including pottery, coins, and sculptures, which provide insights into Rimini's Roman and Etruscan history.

5. Villa Rufolo

Located in nearby Ravello, Villa Rufolo is a historic building that houses a museum and hosts art exhibitions. The villa's beautiful gardens, architecture, and panoramic views have inspired artists and writers throughout history.

6. Emilio Greco Museum

Situated in the city of Orvieto, not far from Rimini, the Emilio Greco Museum is dedicated to the works of the renowned Italian sculptor Emilio Greco. The museum showcases a collection of his sculptures, drawings, and ceramics, offering a comprehensive overview of his artistic career.

7. Museo degli Sguardi (Museum of Glances)

Located in the town of Santarcangelo di Romagna, just a short distance from Rimini, the Museo degli Sguardi is a contemporary art museum housed in a former cinema. It showcases rotating exhibitions of modern and contemporary art, exploring different artistic expressions and perspectives.

8. Museo Fellini
Situated in the town of Gambettola, the Museo Fellini is dedicated to the life and work of Federico Fellini. It offers an intimate look into the personal life of the acclaimed filmmaker through a collection of memorabilia, photographs, and exhibits showcasing the creative process behind his films.

9. Museo della Marineria (Maritime Museum)
Located in Cesenatico, a coastal town near Rimini, the Museo della Marineria is dedicated to the maritime heritage of the region. It features an impressive collection of historical boats, fishing equipment, and exhibits that highlight the relationship between the locals and the sea.

10. Museo del Territorio (Territory Museum)
Situated in the town of Santarcangelo di Romagna, the Museo del Territorio explores the local history, traditions, and cultural identity of the area. It showcases artifacts, photographs, and interactive displays that depict the evolution of the region and its communities.

These museums and galleries provide an opportunity to delve into various aspects of art, history, and culture. Whether you're interested in ancient artifacts, contemporary art, or the cinematic genius of Fellini, these institutions offer a rich and immersive experience in Rimini and its surrounding areas.

Natural Wonders And Parks

Rimini and its surrounding areas are blessed with natural beauty, from stunning coastlines to picturesque parks. Here are some natural wonders and parks to explore during your visit:

1. Parco del Gelso
Located in Rimini's Viserba neighborhood, Parco del Gelso is a charming park characterized by its beautiful mulberry trees. It offers a peaceful environment for a leisurely stroll, picnic, or relaxation amidst nature. The park also features a playground, making it an ideal spot for families.

2. Parco Marecchia
Situated along the Marecchia River, Parco Marecchia is a sprawling park that spans several kilometers. It offers walking and cycling paths, scenic viewpoints, and green spaces where you can enjoy outdoor activities. The park provides a tranquil retreat from the city, with its lush vegetation and river views.

3. Parco Naturale Monte San Bartolo
Located a short distance north of Rimini, Parco Naturale Monte San Bartolo is a protected natural area that showcases the region's stunning coastal landscape. It offers breathtaking views of the Adriatic Sea, rugged cliffs, and pristine beaches. Hiking trails provide an opportunity to explore the park's diverse flora and fauna.

4. Parco del Castello di Montebello
Situated in the town of Montebello, near Rimini, Parco del Castello di Montebello surrounds the ancient Montebello Castle. The park features well-manicured gardens, panoramic viewpoints, and walking paths that lead to the castle ruins. It offers a serene setting to enjoy nature and learn about the area's history.

5. Parco del Mare
Located along Rimini's seafront, Parco del Mare is a waterfront park that combines green spaces with recreational activities. It features walking and cycling paths, playgrounds, fitness areas, and sports facilities. The park offers a lively atmosphere and is a popular spot for locals and tourists alike.

These natural wonders and parks provide opportunities to immerse yourself in Rimini's natural surroundings and enjoy outdoor activities. Whether you prefer a leisurely stroll, a hike along the coast, or a picnic in a serene setting, these natural spaces offer a welcome escape from the urban environment.

Historic Sites And Architecture

Rimini is a city steeped in history, and its architecture reflects its rich cultural heritage. Here are some of the historic sites and architectural gems to visit in Rimini:

1. Malatestiano Bridge (Ponte di Tiberio)
This ancient Roman bridge spans the Marecchia River and is another remarkable architectural feat. Built during the reign of Emperor Augustus, it showcases Roman engineering and offers scenic views of the surrounding area.

2. Church of San Francesco
Located in the historic center of Rimini, the Church of San Francesco is a beautiful medieval church known for its intricate Gothic architecture. It features a stunning rose window and houses notable artworks and frescoes.

3. Palazzo del Governo
Situated in Piazza Cavour, the Palazzo del Governo is a neoclassical building that served as the residence of the Papal Governors during the Papal States era. Its grand facade and elegant interiors make it a notable architectural landmark in the city.

4. Church of Sant'Agostino
This historic church showcases a mix of architectural styles, including Romanesque, Gothic, and Renaissance. Its facade is adorned with beautiful decorations, and the interior houses impressive artworks, such as the Crucifix by Giotto.

5. Arch of the Ponte d'Augusto
Another arch associated with the Roman era, the Arch of the Ponte d'Augusto is located near the Tiberius Bridge. It served as the entrance to the ancient city and is a testament to Rimini's Roman past.

6. Church of Santa Maria dei Servi
This medieval church features a stunning brick facade with intricate details. It is known for its elegant bell tower, which provides a panoramic view of Rimini from the top.

7. Palazzo Bellucci
Located near the Arch of Augustus, Palazzo Bellucci is a historic building with a rich history. It displays architectural elements from different periods, including Gothic and Renaissance styles.

8. Church of San Giovanni Battista

Situated in the Borgo San Giuliano neighborhood, the Church of San Giovanni Battista is a picturesque church with a charming bell tower. Its interior houses beautiful frescoes and artwork.

9. Palazzo Garampi
This neoclassical palace is located in Piazza Cavour and stands out for its elegant facade and architectural details. It currently houses the Rimini City Council.

10. Church of San Giuliano Martire
Situated in the Borgo San Giuliano neighborhood, the Church of San Giuliano Martire is a lovely example of Romanesque architecture. It features a beautiful rose window and houses religious artworks.

These historic sites and architectural treasures provide a glimpse into Rimini's rich history and cultural legacy. Exploring these landmarks will transport you back in time and allow you to appreciate the city's remarkable architecture and its significance throughout the centuries.

Hidden Gems And Local Favorites

Discovering hidden gems and exploring local favorites can add a unique touch to your experience in Rimini.

Here are some lesser-known places and local favorites to consider:

1. Borgo San Giovanni
This charming neighborhood, located outside the city center, offers a more authentic and local atmosphere. Stroll through its narrow streets, visit local shops and cafes, and soak in the laid-back ambiance of this residential area.

2. The Grand Hotel Rimini
While not exactly a hidden gem, the Grand Hotel Rimini is an iconic landmark that has hosted famous guests over the years. Step inside to admire its stunning Art Nouveau architecture and enjoy a drink at its elegant bar.

3. Rimini's Street Art
Take a self-guided tour to explore the vibrant street art scene in Rimini. From colorful murals to thought-provoking graffiti, the city boasts an array of urban art that adds character to its streets.

4. Rimini's Local Markets
Immerse yourself in the local culture by visiting the bustling markets of Rimini. The Mercato Coperto is a covered market where you can find fresh produce, local delicacies, and other goods. The Borgo San Giuliano Market, held on select

weekends, offers a mix of food, crafts, and antiques.

5. Gelato
Indulge in the local favorite dessert, gelato. Rimini is home to numerous gelaterias where you can savor delicious, artisanal gelato in a variety of flavors. Try Gelateria La Romana, Gelateria 3 Bis, or Gelateria Amorino for some delectable frozen treats.

6. Parco Mare Nord
Located in the Viserbella neighborhood, Parco Mare Nord is a peaceful park with a serene lake, walking paths, and picnic spots. It's a hidden gem where you can relax, unwind, and enjoy nature away from the crowds.

7. Piazza Tre Martiri
This historic square, known as the heart of Rimini, is a popular gathering spot for locals. It's lined with cafes and restaurants, making it an ideal place to grab a coffee, people-watch, or simply soak in the vibrant atmosphere.

8. Osteria de Borg
For an authentic taste of local cuisine, head to Osteria de Borg. This cozy restaurant serves traditional dishes, including homemade pasta, seafood specialties, and regional wines. It's a

favorite among locals for its warm ambiance and delicious food.

9. Rimini's Canals
Discover Rimini's network of canals, known as "Fossi," which once played a crucial role in the city's transportation system. Take a leisurely stroll along the canal banks, admire the picturesque views, and capture some beautiful photographs.

10. Fiabilandia
A beloved amusement park among locals, Fiabilandia is an enchanting destination for families. It offers a range of rides, shows, and attractions designed for children, making it a fun-filled day out for the whole family.

Exploring these hidden gems and experiencing local favorites will provide a more intimate and authentic understanding of Rimini's culture, flavors, and hidden corners. Don't be afraid to venture off the beaten path and discover the lesser-known aspects of this captivating city.

Family Friendly Activities In Rimini

Rimini offers a variety of family-friendly activities and attractions that cater to visitors of all ages. Here are some family-friendly activities to enjoy in Rimini:

1. Fiabilandia
Fiabilandia is a popular amusement park designed for families with children. It offers a range of rides, shows, and attractions based on fairy tales and fantasy themes. From gentle rides for younger children to thrilling roller coasters for older kids, Fiabilandia provides a fun-filled day of entertainment.

2. Italia in Miniatura
Italia in Miniatura is a unique theme park that showcases miniature replicas of famous Italian landmarks and attractions. Children can explore the park, marvel at the detailed models, and learn about the country's cultural heritage in an interactive and engaging way.

3. Aquafan
For water lovers, Aquafan is a must-visit water park in Riccione, just a short distance from Rimini. It features a wide range of water slides, pools, and attractions suitable for all ages. The park offers thrilling slides for older kids and adults, as well as dedicated areas for younger children.

4. Beaches
Rimini's sandy beaches provide ample opportunities for family fun. Spend a day building sandcastles, playing beach games, or simply relaxing under the sun. Many beach clubs offer

amenities such as playgrounds, water sports, and entertainment for children.

5. The Dolphinarium
The Rimini Dolphinarium is a captivating place to witness dolphin and sea lion shows. Children can enjoy watching these intelligent creatures perform tricks and learn about marine life through educational presentations.

6. Italy in Wheels
Italy in Wheels is a museum dedicated to vintage cars and motorcycles. It features a collection of classic vehicles that will fascinate car enthusiasts of all ages. The museum offers interactive exhibits and workshops for children to learn about the history and mechanics of these iconic vehicles.

7. Rimini Mini Golf
Engage in a friendly family competition at Rimini Mini Golf. The colorful and challenging mini-golf courses provide hours of entertainment for everyone. It's a great way to enjoy some quality time together and embrace a little friendly rivalry.

8. Rimini's Parks
Rimini boasts several parks and green spaces that are perfect for family outings. Parco del Gelso, Parco del Mare, and Parco Marecchia offer ample space for picnics, bike rides, and

leisurely walks. These parks often have playgrounds, sports facilities, and open areas for kids to run around and enjoy outdoor activities.

9. *Rimini Beach Village*

Rimini Beach Village is a beachside water park that combines water attractions with entertainment for the whole family. It features pools, water slides, and play areas suitable for different age groups. The park also offers organized activities, shows, and games to keep everyone entertained.

10. *Oltremare*

Located in Riccione, Oltremare is an educational and entertaining park focused on nature, animals, and science. It offers interactive exhibits, shows, and attractions that allow visitors to learn about marine life, birds of prey, and other animals.

These family-friendly activities in Rimini provide a range of options to ensure a memorable and enjoyable experience for the whole family. Whether you prefer theme parks, water parks, outdoor adventures, or educational attractions, Rimini has something to offer for every age group.

Day Trips And Excursions From Rimini

Rimini is not only a vibrant city itself but also serves as a convenient base for exploring the surrounding areas. Here are some day trips and excursions you can take from Rimini:

1. San Marino
Just a short distance from Rimini, the independent microstate of San Marino is a must-visit destination. Explore the medieval streets, visit the historic towers and fortresses, and enjoy panoramic views of the surrounding countryside. San Marino offers a unique cultural experience and is known for its picturesque setting.

2. Ravenna
Known for its stunning Byzantine mosaics, Ravenna is a UNESCO World Heritage Site and a treasure trove of art and history. Visit the famous Basilica di San Vitale, Mausoleo di Galla Placidia, and other splendid churches and monuments that showcase exquisite mosaics.

3. Gradara
This medieval village, located about 20 kilometers from Rimini, is famous for its well-preserved castle and picturesque streets.

Take a stroll along the fortress walls, visit the castle, and immerse yourself in the romantic atmosphere of this charming hilltop town.

4. Urbino
Venture into the region of Marche and visit Urbino, a UNESCO World Heritage Site and birthplace of the renowned artist Raphael. Explore the historic center, admire the stunning Ducal Palace, and delve into the city's rich Renaissance heritage.

5. Bologna
Known for its vibrant culinary scene and well-preserved medieval architecture, Bologna is worth a day trip from Rimini. Discover the city's famous leaning towers, stroll through the charming historic center, and savor the local cuisine, including the famous Bolognese sauce.

6. Cesenatico
Located along the Adriatic coast, Cesenatico offers beautiful sandy beaches, a charming canal port, and a vibrant atmosphere. Enjoy a relaxing day at the beach, explore the Maritime Museum, and take a boat ride along the canal to admire the picturesque waterfront.

7. Ferrara
With its well-preserved Renaissance architecture and impressive medieval walls, Ferrara is

another UNESCO World Heritage Site worth exploring. Visit the imposing Estense Castle, wander through the historic center, and immerse yourself in the city's cultural and artistic heritage.

8. Rimini's Hinterland
Discover the picturesque countryside and charming villages of Rimini's hinterland. Visit towns like Santarcangelo di Romagna, Verucchio, and Montegridolfo, known for their medieval architecture, traditional cuisine, and stunning views over the surrounding hills.

9. Modena
Famous for its culinary delights, Modena is a gastronomic paradise. Take a day trip to explore the city's historical center, visit the impressive Modena Cathedral, and indulge in the local specialty, traditional balsamic vinegar.

10. Florence
While Florence is further away from Rimini, it is still possible to visit this iconic Italian city on a day trip if you're willing to travel a bit longer. Explore Florence's renowned art and architecture, including the Uffizi Gallery, Florence Cathedral (Duomo), and Ponte Vecchio.

These day trips and excursions from Rimini offer a diverse range of experiences, from exploring medieval towns to immersing yourself in art and history. Whether you're interested in cultural heritage, natural beauty, or gastronomic delights, there's something for everyone within easy reach of Rimini.

Rimini's Festivals And Carnivals

Several carnivals and festivals take place in Rimini annually. Here are some of them:

1. Rimini Carnival

The Rimini Carnival is a traditional event that takes place in February. It includes colorful parades, masquerade balls, street performances, and live music, creating a festive atmosphere throughout the city.

2. Rimini's Pink Night (La Notte Rosa)

La Notte Rosa is a popular festival that occurs on the first Saturday of July. The entire Adriatic Coast, including Rimini, is transformed into a lively celebration with concerts, fireworks, art installations, and various cultural events. The coastline is illuminated with pink lights, creating a magical ambiance.

3. Rimini International Film Festival

This film festival showcases a diverse selection of national and international films, ranging from independent productions to popular releases. It features screenings, Q&A sessions with filmmakers, and awards ceremonies, attracting film enthusiasts and industry professionals.

4. Rimini International Jazz Festival
Jazz lovers can enjoy a series of jazz concerts and performances by renowned artists from Italy and around the world. The festival features a variety of jazz styles and takes place in various venues throughout Rimini.

5. Rimini International Sand Sculpture Festival
Held during the summer months, this festival showcases impressive sand sculptures created by skilled artists. The sculptures often depict famous landmarks, characters, and themes, and visitors can witness the artists at work and explore the temporary sand art exhibition.

These are just a few examples of the festivals and carnivals that take place in Rimini annually. However, please note that specific dates and details may vary from year to year, so it's recommended to check the official websites or local event listings for the most up-to-date information about these events.

Nightlife In Rimini

Rimini is well-known for its vibrant and energetic nightlife scene. The city offers a wide range of options for those seeking entertainment, including nightclubs, bars, live music venues, and beachfront parties. Here are some highlights of the nightlife in Rimini:

1. Viale Vespucci
This bustling street in Rimini is lined with bars, clubs, and restaurants. It's a popular spot for locals and tourists alike to enjoy a night out. You'll find a variety of establishments offering different music styles and atmospheres.

2. Marina Centro
The Marina Centro area is another vibrant nightlife hub in Rimini. It's home to numerous bars and clubs that cater to different tastes and preferences. You can find anything from trendy cocktail lounges to lively dance clubs playing a mix of music genres.

3. Beach Clubs
Rimini's beachfront is dotted with beach clubs that offer a unique nightlife experience. These clubs often feature DJ sets, live music, and themed parties right on the sand. It's a great way to dance and enjoy the lively atmosphere with the backdrop of the Adriatic Sea.

4. Piazza Cavour
This central square in Rimini is a popular meeting point for locals and visitors. It has a selection of bars and cafes where you can relax and enjoy a drink or aperitivo. The square often

hosts live music performances and outdoor events during the summer months.

5. *Baia Imperiale*
Baia Imperiale is a renowned nightclub located just outside Rimini in the nearby town of Gabicce Mare. It's known for its grand scale, impressive décor, and top-notch DJs. Baia Imperiale attracts a stylish crowd and hosts some of the region's most memorable parties.

6. *Live Music Venues*
Rimini also offers various venues that showcase live music performances. From small jazz clubs to larger concert halls, you can find a range of genres and talented musicians performing throughout the year.

7. *Baia Imperiale*
Baia Imperiale is a renowned nightclub located just outside Rimini in the nearby town of Gabicce Mare. It's known for its grand scale, impressive décor, and top-notch DJs. Baia Imperiale attracts a stylish crowd and hosts some of the region's most memorable parties.

8. *Mojito Beach Club*
Situated on Rimini's beachfront, Mojito Beach Club offers a relaxed and stylish atmosphere. It's a great place to enjoy cocktails, lounge on

sunbeds, and listen to music while taking in the beautiful beach views.

9. Hakuna Matata Beach Club
Another popular beach club in Rimini, Hakuna Matata offers a laid-back and tropical ambiance. It features beachfront seating, live music, DJ sets, and a variety of events throughout the summer season.

10. Molo Street Parade
Molo Street Parade is an annual event held in Rimini, featuring a vibrant parade of floats, street performers, dancers, and music. The parade travels along Rimini's promenade, creating a lively and festive atmosphere.

It's important to note that the nightlife scene in Rimini can be quite lively and bustling, particularly during the summer months. The city attracts a young and energetic crowd, creating a vibrant atmosphere. Remember to check opening hours, dress codes, and any entry requirements for specific venues or events you plan to visit. Also, stay safe.

CHAPTER 4

DINING IN RIMINI

Dining in Rimini offers a delightful culinary experience with a variety of options to satisfy different tastes. From local specialties to international cuisine, there are numerous dining options available throughout the city. Here's an overview of dining options, Rimini's cuisines, and some of the best restaurants, bars, and cafés in the area.

Dining Options

Rimini offers a diverse range of dining options, including:

Restaurants

Rimini has a wide selection of restaurants offering various cuisines such as Italian, seafood, Mediterranean, international, and more. You can find fine dining establishments, family-friendly restaurants, and casual eateries.

Here are the best restaurants in Rimini, along with a brief description of each and their addresses:

   1. Ristorante Pappagallo

Known for its elegant ambiance and attentive service, Ristorante Pappagallo is a top choice for fine dining in Rimini. The restaurant specializes in creative Italian cuisine, blending classic flavors with modern techniques.

Address: Viale Amerigo Vespucci 137, 47921 Rimini RN, Italy.

2. Acqua Salata

This family-run restaurant is renowned for its seafood dishes, particularly its fresh fish caught daily from the Adriatic Sea. The menu features a variety of delicately prepared seafood options, accompanied by a selection of fine wines.

Address: Viale Regina Elena, 205, 47924 Rimini RN, Italy.

3. Osteria de Borg

Situated in the historic center of Rimini, Osteria de Borg captures the essence of Romagnolo cuisine. The restaurant specializes in homemade pasta, savory meat dishes, and traditional desserts, all served in a cozy and welcoming atmosphere.

Address: Via Forzieri, 12, 47921 Rimini RN, Italy.

4. Ristorante La Sangiovesa

La Sangiovesa is known for its excellent wine selection, offering an extensive list of local and regional wines to complement their dishes. The menu features a mix of Italian and international cuisine, showcasing high-quality ingredients.

Address: Piazza Beato Simone Balacchi, 14, 47822 Santarcangelo di Romagna RN, Italy.

5. Ristorante Da Lele
Da Lele is a family-friendly restaurant that serves traditional Italian dishes with a focus on simplicity and quality. Their menu includes homemade pastas, grilled meats, and seasonal specialties.

Address: Via Lagomaggio, 168, 47924 Rimini RN, Italy.

6. Ristorante Il Pesce Innamorato (Il Pesce Innamorato)
This charming restaurant offers a cozy and intimate setting. With a focus on fresh and sustainable seafood, Il Pesce Nella Rete serves delicious seafood dishes, including creative interpretations of classic recipes.

Address: Viale Amerigo Vespucci, 33, 47921 Rimini RN, Italy

These are just a few of the top restaurants in Rimini, known for their exceptional food, ambiance, and service.

Each offers a unique dining experience, showcasing the flavors of the region and beyond. It's always recommended to make reservations in advance, especially during peak seasons, to secure a table at these popular establishments.

Trattorias

Trattorias are traditional Italian eateries that serve authentic regional dishes in a cozy and relaxed atmosphere. They are a great option for experiencing local flavors and homemade Italian cuisine.

We recommend the following Trattorias:

1. Osteria de Borg
Osteria de Borg offers a cozy and rustic atmosphere, reminiscent of a traditional Italian osteria. The menu features a variety of traditional dishes, including homemade pasta, local seafood, and meat specialties. The focus here is on simple, yet flavorful preparations using fresh and high-quality ingredients.

2. *Trattoria da Lele*
Trattoria da Lele is a popular spot among locals and visitors alike. It boasts a warm and welcoming ambiance with attentive service. The trattoria serves classic Italian cuisine, highlighting regional flavors and seasonal ingredients. You can expect to find dishes such

as homemade pasta, risotto, grilled meats, and delectable desserts on their menu.

3. Trattoria L'Alba
Trattoria L'Alba offers a traditional and inviting setting. The trattoria specializes in Emilian cuisine, known for its rich and hearty flavors. You can indulge in dishes like tagliatelle with ragù, tortellini in brodo (broth), and grilled meats. The friendly staff and cozy atmosphere contribute to a memorable dining experience.

4. Trattoria da Paolo
Trattoria da Paolo is a family-run establishment with a reputation for its authentic Italian dishes. The trattoria exudes a warm and convivial atmosphere, making it a great choice for a relaxed meal. The menu features a variety of homemade pasta dishes, fresh seafood, and traditional meat preparations, all prepared with care and attention to detail.

5. Trattoria La Buca
Trattoria La Buca offers a cozy and intimate setting for diners. The trattoria focuses on traditional Romagnolo cuisine, showcasing the flavors and ingredients of the region. From piadina (a local flatbread) and gnocco fritto (fried dough) to hearty meat and fish dishes, Trattoria La Buca aims to deliver a delightful culinary experience.

6. Trattoria Tonino

Trattoria Tonino is known for its welcoming atmosphere and traditional Italian fare. The trattoria offers a diverse menu that includes homemade pasta, fresh seafood, and grilled meats. The dishes are prepared with a combination of traditional techniques and creative flair, resulting in flavorful and satisfying meals.

7. Trattoria Santo Stefano

Trattoria Santo Stefano is a charming trattoria that prides itself on serving authentic regional cuisine. The menu showcases a range of traditional dishes, such as handmade pasta, flavorful sauces, and seasonal specialties. The warm and friendly ambiance adds to the overall dining experience.

8. Trattoria La Casina

Trattoria La Casina offers a cozy and intimate setting for diners. The trattoria focuses on traditional Italian cuisine, with an emphasis on fresh ingredients and homemade preparations. From antipasti to desserts, each dish is crafted with care and attention to detail to create a memorable dining experience.

9. Trattoria del Tempo Perso

Trattoria del Tempo Perso aims to transport diners to a nostalgic era through its traditional decor and culinary offerings. The trattoria specializes in classic Italian dishes, including handmade pasta, succulent meats, and flavorful sauces. The attentive service and warm ambiance contribute to a memorable dining experience.

10. Trattoria La Marianna
Trattoria La Marianna is a cozy and family-friendly trattoria that captures the essence of Italian comfort food. The menu features a variety of traditional dishes, such as hearty soups, homemade pasta, and flavorful meat preparations. The friendly staff and inviting atmosphere make it a great choice for a relaxed meal.

Pizzerias

Italy is renowned for its pizza, and Rimini has no shortage of pizzerias. You can find both traditional and innovative pizza creations made with fresh ingredients and baked in wood-fired ovens.

We recommend the following pizzerias:

1. Pizzeria da Nello

Known for its delicious thin-crust pizzas, Pizzeria da Nello offers a wide range of toppings and flavor combinations. The pizzeria maintains a casual and lively atmosphere, making it a popular choice among locals and tourists.

2. Pizzeria Amarcord
Pizzeria Amarcord is renowned for its authentic Neapolitan-style pizzas. The pizzeria prides itself on using high-quality ingredients and traditional techniques to create pizzas with a perfect balance of flavors. The cozy ambiance adds to the dining experience.

3. Pizzeria 900
Pizzeria 900 is a contemporary pizzeria that offers a diverse selection of wood-fired pizzas. The menu includes both classic and innovative toppings, catering to a variety of preferences. The modern and stylish decor creates a trendy atmosphere.

4. Pizzeria Lo Zodiaco
Pizzeria Lo Zodiaco is a family-run establishment known for its welcoming atmosphere and traditional pizzas. The pizzeria focuses on using fresh, locally sourced ingredients to create flavorsome pizzas that keep customers coming back for more.

5. Pizzeria La Brasserie

Situated near the beach, Pizzeria La Brasserie offers a delightful combination of pizza and seaside ambiance. Alongside classic pizza varieties, they also serve gourmet pizzas with unique toppings. The outdoor seating provides a great view while enjoying your meal.

6. Pizzeria I Butteri
Pizzeria I Butteri is a cozy and rustic pizzeria that specializes in Roman-style thin-crust pizzas. The pizzeria offers a variety of toppings and a friendly, relaxed atmosphere that appeals to both locals and visitors.

7. Pizzeria La Perla
Pizzeria La Perla is known for its traditional Italian pizzas with a focus on simplicity and quality. The pizzeria prides itself on using fresh ingredients and a slow fermentation process to create light and flavorful pizzas.

8. Pizzeria O Sole Mio
Pizzeria O Sole Mio is a popular spot for pizza lovers, offering a variety of classic and gourmet pizzas. The pizzeria uses traditional techniques and high-quality ingredients to ensure a memorable pizza experience.

9. Pizzeria L'Angolo di Napoli
Pizzeria L'Angolo di Napoli specializes in authentic Neapolitan-style pizzas, known for their

soft and chewy crusts. The pizzeria follows traditional recipes and offers a range of traditional toppings, providing a taste of Naples in Rimini.

10. Pizzeria Il Fornaretto

Pizzeria Il Fornaretto is a local favorite, renowned for its wood-fired pizzas made with care and precision. The pizzeria offers a variety of toppings and has a warm and welcoming atmosphere that adds to the overall dining experience.

Seafood Restaurants

Being located on the Adriatic Coast, Rimini is famous for its fresh seafood. There are plenty of seafood restaurants where you can enjoy a variety of dishes featuring fish, shellfish, and other delights from the sea.

We recommend the following seafood restaurants:

1. Ristorante Da Lele

Ristorante Da Lele is known for its fresh seafood dishes and elegant dining experience. The restaurant offers a menu that showcases the flavors of the Adriatic Sea, featuring a variety of fish and shellfish preparations cooked to perfection.

Address: Via Lagomaggio, 168, 47924 Rimini RN, Italy

2. Osteria del Mare

Osteria del Mare is a charming seafood restaurant that combines traditional and contemporary flavors. The menu highlights locally sourced seafood, allowing guests to savor the freshest catches prepared with a creative twist.

Address: Viale Regina Margherita, 75, 47924 Rimini RN, Italy

3. Il Portolotto

Il Portolotto is known for its refined seafood cuisine and breathtaking views of the harbor. The restaurant offers a range of seafood delicacies, expertly crafted with a focus on quality ingredients and artistic presentation.

Address: Via Lucio Lando, 22, 47921 Rimini RN, Italy

4. Bar ristorante Tripoli

Bar ristorante Tripoli is a charming seafood trattoria known for its rustic and homey ambiance. The menu features a variety of seafood options, including fresh fish, shellfish, and traditional seafood pasta dishes, prepared with care and passion.

Address: Lungomare Augusto Murri, 16, 47921 Rimini RN, Italy

5. Ristorante L'Angolo di Mario

Ristorante L'Angolo di Mario is a family-run seafood restaurant known for its warm hospitality and delectable seafood dishes. The menu features a variety of fresh seafood options, prepared with traditional recipes and served in a cozy atmosphere.

Address: Lungomare Nazario Sauro, 61121 Pesaro PU, Italy.

Rimini's Cuisines

Rimini offers a variety of delicious cuisines that are worth exploring. Here are some of Rimini's notable cuisines

1. Romagnolo Cuisine

Romagnolo cuisine is a prominent culinary tradition in Rimini, known for its hearty and flavorful dishes. You can find traditional Romagnolo cuisine in trattorias and osterias throughout the city.

2. Seafood Cuisine

Being a coastal city, Rimini is renowned for its fresh seafood dishes. Numerous seafood restaurants in Rimini offer a wide range of delectable options.

3. Pizza
Italy is famous for its pizza, and Rimini has a great selection of pizzerias that serve mouth watering pizzas.

4. Gelato
Gelato, Italian-style ice cream, is a must-try dessert in Rimini. You can find gelaterias throughout the city, offering a wide variety of flavors.

5. Emilian Cuisine
Rimini is located in the Emilia-Romagna region, known for its rich culinary heritage. Emilian cuisine features dishes like fresh pasta, Parmigiano-Reggiano cheese, and cured meats.

These are just a few examples of the cuisines. The city offers a wide range of culinary experiences, and exploring the local trattorias, osterias, and restaurants will allow you to discover even more delicious dishes and flavors.

Best Bars In Rimini

Here are some popular bars in Rimini where you can enjoy a drink and socialize:

1. Rock Island Pub
Rock Island Pub is a lively bar that offers a great atmosphere with live music, DJs, and a dance floor. They serve a wide range of drinks, including beers, cocktails, and spirits.

2. Molo Street Parade
Molo Street Parade is a vibrant bar and nightclub located near the beach. It hosts themed parties and events and offers a mix of music genres, including EDM, hip-hop, and house. They have a spacious outdoor area and a variety of drinks to choose from.

3. Bambù Beach Bar
Bambù Beach Bar is a popular beachfront bar known for its relaxed atmosphere and scenic views. It's an ideal spot to enjoy a cocktail or a refreshing drink while soaking up the sun.

4. Bounty Pub Rimini
Bounty Pub Rimini is a lively Irish pub that offers a wide selection of beers, spirits, and cocktails. It's a popular spot for live sports broadcasts, and they often have live music performances.

5. Coconuts Rimini
Coconuts Rimini is a beachfront bar known for its tropical vibe and laid-back ambiance. They serve a variety of cocktails, including their signature

coconut-based drinks. It's a perfect spot to relax and enjoy a drink with friends.

6. *Vanilla Club*
Vanilla Club is a renowned nightclub that attracts both locals and tourists. It features multiple dance floors with different music styles, including EDM, R&B, and commercial hits. They also have a bar area serving a wide range of drinks.

7. *La Cantinaccia di Rimini*
La Cantinaccia di Rimini is a cozy wine bar known for its extensive wine selection. They offer a variety of regional and international wines, accompanied by a selection of cheese and cured meats.

Please note that the availability and offerings of these establishments change. It's always a good idea to check for the latest information, reviews, and operating hours before visiting.

CHAPTER 5

SHOPPING IN RIMINI

Rimini offers a diverse shopping scene, ranging from popular shopping areas to specialty stores and boutiques. Here are some highlights of the shopping experience in Rimini:

Popular Shopping Areas

1. **Corso d'Augusto**
   Located in the heart of Rimini, Corso d'Augusto is a bustling street lined with shops, boutiques, and department stores. Here, you can find a wide range of fashion brands, accessories, and household items.

2. **Via Regina Margherita**
   Another popular shopping street in Rimini, Via Regina Margherita offers a mix of fashion boutiques, shoe stores, and specialty shops. It's a great place to explore and find trendy clothing and accessories.

3. **Viale Vespucci**
   Viale Vespucci is a vibrant street that runs parallel to the beach in Rimini. It is lined with

shops, boutiques, and stores where you can find clothing, accessories, beachwear, and more. The street offers a mix of both international and local brands, making it a popular shopping destination.

4. *Viale Tripoli*
Viale Tripoli is another bustling street in Rimini that offers a variety of shopping options. You can find a range of shops selling clothing, shoes, accessories, and other items. It's a great place to explore and discover new fashion trends.

5. *Centro Commerciale "I Malatesta"*
Located in the suburb of Santa Giustina, Centro Commerciale "I Malatesta" is a large shopping center that houses numerous stores, including fashion retailers, electronics shops, beauty salons, and more. It offers a wide range of options for shopping, dining, and entertainment.

6. *Centro Commerciale "Auchan"*
Situated in the nearby town of Savignano sul Rubicone, Centro Commerciale "Auchan" is a popular shopping center that attracts both locals and visitors from Rimini. It features a variety of shops, including fashion stores, supermarkets, home goods stores, and restaurants.

7. *Piazza Tre Martiri*

Piazza Tre Martiri is a historic square in Rimini that not only offers a charming ambiance but also hosts various shops and boutiques. Here, you can find a mix of local businesses selling clothing, accessories, jewelry, and more. It's a great place to wander and explore unique finds.

Souvenirs and Local Crafts

1. **Borgo San Giuliano**
   This picturesque neighborhood is known for its narrow streets and vibrant colors. It's a great place to find unique souvenirs and local crafts, including handmade ceramics, artwork, and traditional products.

2. **Mercato Coperto**
   Located in the city center, Mercato Coperto is a covered market where you can find local food products, fresh produce, and regional specialties. It's a great spot to pick up ingredients for cooking or sample local delicacies.

3. **Centro Storico (Historic Center)**
   The historic center of Rimini is a treasure trove for finding unique souvenirs and local crafts. The narrow streets are dotted with charming shops and boutiques that sell handmade ceramics, artisanal products, local artwork, and traditional crafts.

4. **Mercato Settimanale di Marina Centro**
   Held every Wednesday in Piazzale Kennedy, Mercato Settimanale di Marina Centro is a weekly market where you can discover a variety of items, including clothing, accessories, household goods, and local food products. It's a great place to find affordable souvenirs and local specialties.

5. **Borgo San Giovanni**
   Located just outside the city center, Borgo San Giovanni is a lively neighborhood known for its local atmosphere. Here, you can find small shops and artisan studios where you can purchase handmade crafts, jewelry, and unique souvenirs.

6. **Rimini Fiera (Trade Fair)**
   Rimini Fiera is a large exhibition center that hosts various trade fairs and events throughout the year. These events often feature local artisans and craftsmen who showcase their products, including ceramics, textiles, leather goods, and more. It's an excellent opportunity to explore and support local artisans.

7. **Rimini Sunday Market**
   Held every Sunday in the Viserba neighborhood, the Rimini Sunday Market is a vibrant street market where you can find a wide range of items, including clothing, accessories, home decor,

vintage goods, and local crafts. It's a lively and bustling market that offers a unique shopping experience.

Fashion and Design

1. **Le Befane Shopping Center**
   Situated on the outskirts of Rimini, Le Befane is a large shopping center with a variety of fashion stores, electronics shops, and entertainment options. It offers a one-stop shopping experience for fashion and lifestyle needs.

2. **Piazza Cavour**
   In the heart of Rimini, Piazza Cavour is surrounded by elegant boutiques and high-end fashion stores. Here, you can find renowned Italian and international brands, as well as luxury goods and accessories.

3. **Viale Vespucci**
   Viale Vespucci, running along the beachfront, is not only popular for its shopping options but also for its fashion and design stores. You can find a variety of fashion boutiques and concept stores offering clothing, accessories, and footwear from both local and international brands.

4. **Via Dante**
   Located in the heart of Rimini, Via Dante is a charming street that boasts a mix of fashion

boutiques and design stores. Here, you can find trendy clothing, unique accessories, and stylish home decor items.

5. **Piazzale Fellini**
Piazzale Fellini, situated near Rimini's promenade, is a popular area known for its fashionable shops. It offers a blend of renowned Italian brands, designer labels, and upscale fashion stores. You can explore the latest trends in clothing, accessories, and luxury goods.

6. **C.so d'Augusto**
C.so d'Augusto, mentioned earlier as a popular shopping street, is also a hub for fashion and design. Along this vibrant avenue, you'll find a range of fashion boutiques, shoe stores, and design shops where you can discover unique pieces and trendy fashion items.

7. **Le Befane Shopping Center**
While not a specific area, Le Befane Shopping Center deserves a mention for its extensive fashion and design offerings. This large shopping center features numerous fashion retailers, both local and international, offering a wide selection of clothing, footwear, accessories, and home decor items.

Markets and Flea Markets

1. Mercato di Rimini

Held every Wednesday and Saturday in Piazzale Kennedy, Mercato di Rimini is a bustling open-air market. It offers a wide range of items, including clothing, accessories, fresh produce, and household goods.

2. Mercatino dell'Antiquariato

This antique market takes place in Piazza Cavour on the third Sunday of every month. It's a treasure trove for antique enthusiasts, offering a selection of vintage items, furniture, artwork, and collectibles.

Specialty Stores and Boutiques

1. Gelateria Romana

Located in the historic center, Gelateria Romana is a renowned gelato shop that offers a variety of delicious flavors. It's a must-visit for ice cream lovers and those seeking authentic Italian gelato.

2. Enoteca Tognoni

This wine shop specializes in Italian wines and offers a wide selection of regional and international labels. It's a great place to explore and purchase quality wines as souvenirs or for personal enjoyment.

3. ***Ottica Cerioni***
   If you're looking for stylish eyewear, Ottica Cerioni is a reputable optical store in Rimini. They offer a range of designer frames, sunglasses, and optical services.

These are just a few examples of the shopping options available in Rimini. Whether you're looking for fashion, souvenirs, local crafts, or specialty items, Rimini has something to offer for every shopper.

CHAPTER 6

OTHER PRACTICAL INFORMATION

Here is other practical information to take note of while planning your trip.

Money Matters

Currency

The currency used in Rimini, as well as throughout Italy, is the Euro (€).

Money Exchange

You can exchange your currency for Euros at banks, exchange offices, or at the airport. It's advisable to compare exchange rates and fees to ensure you get the best deal.

ATMs

ATMs (Bancomat) are widely available in Rimini, allowing you to withdraw cash using your debit or credit card. Check with your bank regarding any international transaction fees or withdrawal limits.

Credit Cards

Major credit cards such as Visa, MasterCard, and American Express are widely accepted in hotels, restaurants, and shops in Rimini. However, it's always a good idea to carry some cash for smaller establishments and in case of emergencies.

Language and Communication

Language

The official language of Rimini, as well as the rest of Italy, is Italian. English is spoken to some extent in tourist areas, hotels, and restaurants, but it's helpful to learn a few basic Italian phrases.

Useful Phrases

Here are a few useful Italian phrases:
- Hello: Ciao
- Thank you: Grazie
- Yes: Sì
- No: No
- Excuse me: Mi scusi
- Do you speak English?: Parla inglese?
- I need help: Ho bisogno di aiuto
- Where is...?: Dove si trova...?
- How much does it cost?: Quanto costa?

Travel Insurance and Health Concerns

Travel Insurance

It's recommended to have travel insurance that covers medical expenses, trip cancellations, and lost or stolen belongings. Check with your insurance provider to ensure you have adequate coverage.

Health Concerns

Rimini generally has good healthcare facilities. However, it's advisable to have travel insurance that covers medical expenses. European Union citizens should carry a European Health Insurance Card (EHIC) for access to medical services.

Safety and Security

Rimini is considered a relatively safe city for travelers. However, it's always important to take general precautions to ensure your safety. Be cautious of your belongings, avoid walking alone in dimly lit areas at night, and stay aware of your surroundings.

Travel Warnings

Stay informed about travel warnings or advisories issued by your government or relevant authorities for the region you plan to visit. It's essential to be aware of any potential risks or concerns before your trip.

Emergency Contacts

- Emergency Services: In case of emergencies, dial the following numbers:
- Police: 112
- Medical Emergencies: 118
- Fire Department: 115

Remember to have important contact numbers, including your embassy or consulate, saved in case of any emergencies or assistance required during your stay.

It's always a good idea to check for the most up-to-date information and consult official sources before traveling to Rimini or any other destination.

CHAPTER 7

CONCLUSION

In conclusion, Rimini offers a captivating blend of history, culture, beautiful beaches, delicious cuisine, and vibrant atmosphere. This travel guide has provided you with valuable insights into the city's top attractions, must-visit landmarks, renowned restaurants, and popular shopping areas. Whether you're a history enthusiast, a beach lover, a foodie, or a fashion enthusiast, Rimini has something to offer for everyone.

Explore the ancient ruins of the Roman Empire, soak up the sun on the sandy beaches, indulge in the delectable local cuisine, and immerse yourself in the lively atmosphere of this charming Italian city. From the iconic Arch of Augustus to the bustling streets of Viale Vespucci, Rimini's rich heritage and modern offerings make it a memorable destination.

Remember to embrace the Italian way of life, savoring every moment, indulging in local traditions, and taking the time to connect with the friendly locals. Whether you're strolling through the historic center, enjoying a gelato by the sea, or sipping a cappuccino at a local café, Rimini promises to leave you with unforgettable memories.

As you embark on your journey to Rimini, be prepared with practical information about currency exchange, language tips, transportation options, and emergency contacts. With this knowledge in hand, you can navigate the city with ease and enjoy a worry-free experience.

We hope this travel guide has sparked your wanderlust and provided you with the inspiration and information needed to make the most of your trip to Rimini. May your journey be filled with incredible experiences, cultural discoveries, and moments of pure joy as you explore the captivating city of Rimini.

Additional Resources

Below is a list of The Most Visited Travel and Tourism Websites which would aid you in finding whatever you need in regards to your travel to not just Rimini, but anywhere else nationally and internationally. From accommodation arrangements to transportation bookings and everything else in-between, the following sites will assist you. Not all of the sites support Rimini related aid, but a good number of them do.

1. booking.com
2. tripadvisor.com
3. airbnb.com
4. expedia.com
5. agoda.com
6. uber.com
7. southwest.com

8. jalan.net
9. aa.com
10. navitime.co.jp
11. vrbo.com
12. hotels.com
13. marriott.com
14. ryanair.com
15. delta.com
16. travel.rakuten.co.jp
17. makemytrip.com
18. kayak.com
19. united.com
20. skyscanner.net
21. irctc.co.in
22. tripadvisor.co.uk
23. thetrainline.com
24. hilton.com
25. rome2rio.com
26. bahn.de
27. trip.com
28. priceline.com
29. tutu.ru
30. flightaware.com
31. eastday.com
32. adanione.com
33. viator.com
34. latamairlines.com
35. klook.com
36. tripadvisor.in
37. ikyu.com
38. indianrail.gov.in

39. tripadvisor.it
40. tripadvisor.fr
41. easyjet.com
42. tripadvisor.es
43. ana.co.jp
44. tfl.gov.uk
45. jal.co.jp
46. travelandleisure.com
47. ihg.com
48. mta.info
49. aircanada.com
50. airbnb.co.uk

Buon viaggio!

Printed in Great Britain
by Amazon